C000024417

Contents

Acknowledgements

We are indebted to Carole Bird who painstakingly spent many hours typing the manuscript, to Patricia Shannon who helped with the proof reading and to all the secretarial staff who typed up initial drafts and bore with all the numerous re-writes before individual contributors were satisfied with their submissions. We are also grateful for the help and encouragement from professional colleagues both in Somerset and Kent. Particular thanks also to Adrian Faupel whose helpful comments during the preparation of the chapter on groupwork were much appreciated.

We acknowledge all the children whose poetry, artwork and comments helped to develop our insights in this difficult area and provided such an inspiration, especially the poetry of Anna Dinnage and John Green, the cover illustration by Josh Wyles and the pictures which were created as part of the *Mapping the Environment and Self Project* by the children of Hotwells Primary School, Bristol, with the help of the Artist in Residence, Glyn Wyles. The project was funded by the Gulbenkian Foundation, July 1991.

How to Cope with Childhood Stress: A Practical Guide for Teachers

Edited by

Pippa Alsop
and
Trisha McCaffrey

LONGMAN

Published by Longman Information & Reference,
Longman Group UK Ltd, Westgate House, The High,
Harlow, Essex CM20 1YR, UK.
Telephone (0279) 442601
Fax: (0279) 444501

First published 1993

A catalogue record for this book is available from the British
Library

ISBN 0 582 21953 1

Typeset by EMS Phototypesetting, Berwick upon Tweed.

Printed in Great Britain by BPCC Wheatons Ltd, Exeter

List of contributors

Pippa Alsop   Principal Medical Social Worker, Somerset County Council working with the Taunton and Somerset NHS Trust.

Dr Alan Cockett   Consultant Child and Adolescent Psychiatrist, Avalon Somerset NHS Trust.

Heather Collins   Senior Educational Psychologist Somerset County Council.

Dr Martyn Gay   Consultant Child and Adolescent Psychiatrist, United Bristol Healthcare NHS Trust.

Dr Jean Harris Hendriks   Consultant Psychiatrist, Child and Family Service, South Bedfordshire Community Health Care Trust.

David Knapman   Senior Educational Psychologist, Somerset County Council.

Annabel Martin   Senior Paediatric Social Worker, Somerset County Council working with the Taunton and Somerset NHS Trust.

Trisha McCaffrey   Senior Educational Psychologist, Kent County Council.

Haley Moore   Alcohol Education Co-ordinator, Somerset Health Authority.

David Pollard   Drug Services Co-ordinator, Somerset Council on Alcohol and Drugs.

Madeleine Thomas   Top Grade Clinical Psychologist, Head of Psychology (Learning Difficulties) Service, Avalon Somerset NHS Trust.

Dr Annick Vogels   Clinical Assistant in Child and Adolescent Psychiatry, United Bristol Healthcare NHS Trust.

The poetry

John Green   whose poetry is included in this book, is a black boy of Nigerian descent. He has had a very traumatic early history and has spent much time in care.

He suffers from asthma, eczema, rhinitis and scoliosis. He has slightly impaired vision and poor visual memory. He is not comfortable with a black identity and emotional problems and physical difficulties together with a stressful life have led to chronic self-neglect. Despite these difficulties, John is exceptionally talented in some areas and was pleased to be able to contribute to this book as a way of helping teachers to understand the stresses that face pupils like him.

About the editors

Pippa Alsop qualified as a social worker in Bristol in 1974 since which time she has worked in community and health settings. For the past ten years she has been Principal Social Worker working for Somerset County Council with the Taunton and Somerset N.H.S. Trust where she heads a team of social workers who work in general hospitals.

For many years she has had an interest in helping bereaved families and in particular helping people who have been bereaved suddenly and through suicide. She was a founder member of Cruse Bereavement Care in Somerset and is the Southern Representative on their National Council. She has lectured locally and nationally on issues related to terminal illness and bereavement.

Trisha McCaffrey left teaching in 1980 to read psychology at Lancaster University, going to Southampton University for professional training. She obtained a Masters degree in Educational Psychology in 1986. In May 1992 she was appointed Specialist Senior Educational Psychologist in East Kent, a joint Education and Social Services appointment in response to the 1989 Children Act. Part of her brief includes interagency child protection. Prior to that she worked for the best part of six years as an educational psychologist in Somerset, taking a particular interest in developing strategies to support children who are stressed as a result of abusive experiences or traumatic life events.

Introduction

The editors were prompted to look at the literature which was available on childhood stress during the build-up to the Gulf War. At this time, through their work, they became aware that teachers were very concerned that in a large scale conflict, with many casualties, they would be overwhelmed by the need to support traumatised children. Most of the publications seemed to deal either with the research evidence, or to be directed at professional therapeutic interventions. There are from time-to-time, tragedies within the lives of the children we teach in schools. They do not necessarily attract global or national publicity, but they are, nonetheless, seriously emotionally disabling for the young people involved at the time. The editors felt that advice directed at these issues would help teachers feel that they could not only offer appropriate help within the classroom, but also have a good understanding of how and when to enlist the support of appropriate outside agencies.

People do not normally practise handling traumatic situations in the course of their daily lives. Sometimes we hear of very sad circumstances which relate to someone of our acquaintance. We are unlikely to know how to approach them, we may be unsure whether we should mention what has happened, we even avoid them in order to avoid a social gaffe, and these situations can be reflected in school life also. A teacher, on hearing of a bereavement, a family breakdown or abuse, may be unsure how best to help the pupil concerned, or how to deal with the isolation they observe as the peer group struggles with the same problem. Hopefully, in these chapters, the reader will develop their understanding and pick up some practical ideas that can make a real difference to the children concerned.

What is stress?

Stress is usually taken to mean the unpleasant experience of over or under stimulation which will actually or potentially lead to ill health. In the case of children, it may also lead to a failure to develop.

No human being can function without stimulation and challenge. It is a normal part of life and provides excitement, impetus and motivation as well as distress and anxiety. As long as you are able to feel in control, challenge can be invigorating and exciting. The term 'stress' is usually used to describe the mismatch between the challenges you experience and the belief you have in your ability to cope with them. Stress is cumulative so that a series of minor stresses can generate disabling emotions such as overwhelming anxiety and tension, difficulty in thinking clearly and a wide range of behavioural responses. Stress in children is in many ways similar to stress in adults; where it may differ is in its presentation. We are often poor at recognising the signs and symptoms of stress in ourselves or our colleagues, and recognising the signs that a child is experiencing stress can often be even more difficult in children, whose means of communication are restricted and whose understanding of their internal and external worlds is limited.

There are periods in a child's life which are 'normally' more stressful than their previous experience, starting a new school or progressing through adolescence, for example. Individuals show a great deal of variation in how they cope with the stresses and strains of life and some adopt coping strategies which are helpful and effective in the short term, only becoming dysfunctional when they are continued long after the problem has passed. Sometimes children select inappropriate coping strategies which they, because of their immature understanding of the world, believe are helping to solve their problems, which in fact will be likely to lead them to further distress. Children are unlikely to be able to articulate the stress they feel, and they are more likely to show that they have a problem through their behaviour.

There is now a lot of evidence that stress can have a serious effect on the health and wellbeing of individuals. Links have been established between the severity of certain juvenile conditions such as rheumatoid arthritis, diabetes, cancer and cystic fibrosis and the stress that the individual is experiencing. In a book on life events as stressors in childhood and adolescence, Johnson (1986) reports studies indicating that stress is associated with a wide range of health issues including not only physical problems and chronic illness, but also the frequency of accidents.

Stress is a particular problem in childhood because so much of a child's life and environment is controlled by adults. Children can often be left feeling that they can do nothing about their situation, that their position is totally powerless. This in turn leads to feelings of apathy and a loss of all motivation. Poor motivation and lack of self esteem are often consequences of unrecognised stress within the child which they themselves have been unable to deal with effectively, and this has left them feeling disabled and inadequate.

Although there are many parallels between adult stress and that found in children, it is also true to say that children live in a very different world in many ways to the world of adults and the things that trouble and distress them will reflect that difference. Children to a large extent have their lives controlled and managed by adults. This lack of self control over life events, makes children feel particularly vulnerable. If you also add into the equation their conceptual immaturities and misperceptions, then it is easy to see why they can be so adversely affected by circumstances beyond their control.

Equally, adults need to be cautioned that there can be a mismatch between our adult perceptions of the impact of life events and those of children. Studies in the United States and in the United Kingdom of the effects of life-event changes on the stress levels of children, demonstrate that the child's appraisal of stressful events is likely to change with increasing maturity. Other factors that will influence the impact of the stressful life event will be such things as the child's ability to conceptualise the event, their self esteem and the messages they are receiving from significant others about the degree of threat posed by that particular event.

Life event stresses are normally known to significant adults in the child's life, and there is often potential for enlisting adult sympathy and support. Daily life stresses on the other hand can often be more difficult to identify and the behavioural consequences more difficult for adults to understand. Jane Madders (1987) worked with a junior school class and their peers to compile a list of stresses which included both life events and daily stresses. The ranking of stressful events by these children led to some useful, if unexpected, insights.

Ranking of stressful events

1. Loss of parent (death or divorce)
2. Wetting in class
3. Getting lost; being left alone
4. Being bullied by older children
5. Last for the team
6. Ridiculed in class
7. Parental rows
8. Moving to a new class or school

9. Going to dentist/hospital
10. Tests and exams
11. Taking home a bad report
12. Breaking or losing things
13. Being different (accent or clothes)
14. New baby in the family
15. Performing in public
16. Being late for school

One can see from this list how important daily life stresses are in children's lives. Note for example that wetting in class rates as the second highest concern, and that by comparison a new baby in the family comes in fourteenth place. This emphasises the point that for a school-aged child, things that single them out negatively from their peers, or are perceived by the child to do so, provoke the highest levels of anxiety and stress.

The strong focus on school centred activities as a source of daily stresses for all children can be seen as encouraging, as at least these are areas in which teachers can have some influence.

Researchers have also identified the fact that some children are more vulnerable to stress than others. Being of an ethnic minority or having cultural differences may powerfully affect children's ability to benefit from peer group support and, taken in conjunction with other forms of disadvantage, may make them particularly vulnerable.

Werner (1985) found that sociability which can elicit positive attention from care-givers, and communication skills, which enable children to enlist adult support when needed, were associated with resilience at all ages from infancy to adulthood. Boys are reported to be more stressed in childhood, whilst girls report more stress in adolescence. Boys are more likely to respond to stress with destructive behaviour, but girls, who have no competent female role model, who are under high levels of stress, will also respond disruptively (Masten 1988). Masten also found that whereas stress did not affect the achievement of children with high IQs, it did affect the achievement of children of lower ability.

Interpersonal variables, particularly those affecting family functioning, can also strongly influence a child's response to stress; for example, the finding that parental, especially maternal, competence, affects girls' ability to respond to high levels of stress; also the finding that infants who are strongly attached to their parents would cope with separation better than those who have weak attachments. The protective effect of high quality relationships within the family has been found to extend into adolescence.

Where children feel that they have some control over their lives without having to take on adult responsibilities, they experience less stress. Personal competence and good social supports (friendship and peer group activities) that children enjoy have been shown to have a profound effect on their ability to cope with stress. When personal competence and social support are considered together they are more powerful than either on its own.

A positive school ethos and whole school behaviour policy can have a considerable influence on fostering resilience and reducing stress for pupils. Legislation (the Children Act, 1989) places much emphasis on putting 'children first'. Most teachers would undoubtedly assert that they already do this, but putting children first does not just mean committing one's life to working with and for them. It means putting children's needs before operational and logistic consideration, being flexible and responsive; providing structures and boundaries which enable children to feel secure and safe within the rules and routines of school life. We need to consider how we can give children the right to have their basic emotional and developmental needs met, without passing on to them the responsibility to ensure that this happens. Achieving this balance may be the most significant contributor to that lauded but elusive quality 'a positive school ethos'. School children spend the majority of their waking lives in our schools, and teachers are in a powerful position to have a significant effect on whether a child copes with their experiences in a constructive way.

Teachers are not responsible for dealing with all the trauma in a child's life, but through understanding they can sometimes reduce a child's distress. Conventional wisdom dictates that childhood is a happy time, a time of warm summer afternoons with new mown grass, daisy chains and sports days. Not all our children will look back on their childhood with fond recollections like these; but for all of them there will be recollections of teachers who have made a significant difference to their lives. Our own histories are a testament to this. Teachers matter, and what teachers do can matter very much.

References

Arnold L E 1990 *Childhood stress*. John Wiley & Sons

Johnson J H, McCutchion S, 1980, Assessing life stress in older children and adolescents: preliminary findings with the life events checklist. In Sarason I G, Spielberger C D (eds) *Stress and anxiety*, New York, Hemisphere.

Johnson J H 1986, Life event stressors in childhood and adolescence. Sage Publications

Madders J 1987 *Relax and be happy.* Union Paperbacks

Mains B, Robinson G 1992 *The no blame approach.* The Lame Duck Publishing

Masten A S *et al* 1988 Competence and stress in school children: the moderating effect of individual and family qualities. *Journal of Child Psychology and Psychiatry* **29** (6)

Rutter M 1979 Protective factors in children's responses to stress and disadvantage. In Kent M W, Rolf J E (eds) *Primary prevention of psychopathology.* University Press of New England

Werner E E 1985 Stress and protective factors in children's lives. In Nichol A R (ed) *Longitudinal studies in child psychology and psychiatry.* Wiley

Colour of my skin

Man with no white skin
You're easy to see and the skin that
You're scratching makes me hate me.

I ain't the spine that you're hating
Nor your souls bright spark
It's your skin that you're scratching
So greasy and dark.

I have an Afro, no long flowing hair
My friends make no big deal but I still care
I love dark hair and blue eyes
I'd rather be them
I'd be those not them and no longer condemned.

John Green

1 Child protection: innocent lives

Introduction

For centuries children have been murdered, sent into slavery and abused. It was not, however, until the early 1970s that child abuse became recognised and tested, perhaps through the death of a little girl called Maria Colwell, who, having been returned to her parents after six years in foster care, was battered to death by her stepfather. Maria's case highlighted the plight of children who are not understood and die because of ignorance. Increasing numbers of children died in the 1980s and a number of inquiries ensued. These deaths have made local authorities, health authorities and voluntary organisations look at their practice as far as children's needs are concerned and much preventative work has been done which now means that very few children die. Several thousand children however are known to be abused each year in a variety of ways by their families, carers, friends, acquaintances and strangers.

In some areas teachers will never meet abused children but in others, particularly in inner cities, they may experience abuse more often. It is a very emotive subject and it is therefore very important that teachers and support staff in educational establishments know what to look for and what to do if they suspect abuse.

What is child abuse?

Children can be abused in many ways but the definition is usually divided into four categories:

1. Physical injury
2. Neglect
3. Sexual abuse
4. Emotional abuse

Physical injury

Physical injury can range from extreme discipline, slapping, shaking, punching, burning and deliberately injuring a child in a physical way. Most children who have died have died as a result of deliberate physical injury by parents or other carers.

Neglect

Neglect can range from ignoring a child's developmental needs to not feeding or clothing them adequately and leaving a young child unsupervised. Teachers should be particularly aware of the warning signs. These may include: voracious appetite at school, stealing food from other children, dry, sparse hair, developmental delay, unresponsiveness or frozen watchfulness, indiscriminate relationships with adults, short stature and underweight for chronological age, swollen limbs with pitted sores that are slow to heal and poor skin condition.

Sexual abuse

Sexual abuse is the involvement of dependent developmentally immature children and young people in sexual activities they do not comprehend and to which they are unable to give formal consent or that violate social taboos or family roles. This can include inappropriate touching, pornography, as well as attempted or actual sexual intercourse.

Emotional abuse

Emotional abuse is usually very difficult to identify but is the severe adverse affect on the behaviour and emotional development of a child caused by persistent or severe emotional ill treatment or rejection.

It should be noted that children can be abused in a variety of ways which may include one or more of the categories.

Other indications of abuse

When considering if a child might have been abused a number of other factors should be taken into account. Research suggests that child abuse is more likely to occur in families with certain characteristics. Identification of these families may help in preventative work. These characteristics may add to the suspicion of abuse but do not prove it.

They include parents who are young without a settled lifestyle, who are socially isolated with poor inter-personal relationships; parents who have experienced aggression, abuse, disruption or rejection in their own childhood; parents who are under stress because of finances, overcrowding and poor living conditions; parents who are immature and highly emotional and may be dependent on drink or drugs; parents of limited intelligence and with a history of mental ill health and also in a situation where one parent is not the biological parent of the child.

The interdisciplinary approach to child protection

At a local level all areas have an Area Child Protection Committee which provides a joint forum for developing, monitoring and reviewing child protection policies. Child protection committees issue guidelines which are available to all professionals which state procedures for identifying, investigating and reviewing children who are abused. All educational establishments will have access to a copy of these guidelines, either available through the head-teacher or a senior member of staff designated to handle child protection issues also known as the child protection co-ordinator. It is very important that all teaching and support staff should familiarise themselves with these guidelines so that should there be any suspicion that a child is being abused or if a child discloses abuse to a member of staff, they know what course of action they should take.

These guidelines take the reader through the whole process of responses to child abuse including definitions of abuse, how referrals are made, right through to child protection case conferences, court proceedings and reviewing.

The prime responsibility for the care and protection of abused children lies with the local authority social services department. Referrals can, however, be made to the police and the National Society for the Prevention of Cruelty to Children. It is likely that in a situation where abuse is suspected by a teacher or support member of staff in schools the main referring point will be the social services department through the designated staff member or child protection co-ordinator. Most local authority schools will have links either through the education welfare officer, the school social worker or the educational psychologist with the local authority social services and this contact can certainly aid the referring process as hopefully trust will already be well established between agencies.

The Children Act 1989

October 1991 saw the full implementation of the Children Act 1989, a far-reaching new framework which endeavours to ensure the care and protection of children.

The key elements of the Act are that the child's welfare is paramount and that local authorities should work in partnership with parents where possible to allow children to remain in their families by voluntary agreement. Compulsory action would only be indicated through the courts if it was thought to be in the best interests of the child.

National guidelines, namely HMSO, *Working together under the Children Act 1989*, are available and give information to education staff on their role and the processes expected around child protection issues.

The role of staff working in the education service with reference to child protection

Staff working in educational establishments, both in the public and private sectors, will have a key role to play in the early identification of children who are being abused or who are suspected of having been abused. Teachers and support staff usually see children far more often than other professionals and should be in a position to observe signs of physical abuse, sexual abuse, neglect and emotional abuse. Teachers will also have a role to play where there is already proven abuse and the child is remaining in a family or with carers. They should be on the alert for signs of distress, emotional deprivation and significant changes in a child's behaviour.

If a teacher or support member of staff suspects a child in their care is being abused in any way it is important that they report it immediately to the headteacher or to the school's child protection co-ordinator, who would then alert the local social services department who will initiate procedures in collaboration with other key agencies.

It is important that the area child protection committee's

guidelines are strictly followed.

In the case of physical injury or a serious threat to the child's safety, the most important factor is to ensure that the child is safe and will not be in a position where they will be subjected to more abuse. If a child presents at school with injuries which need medical attention the school should immediately seek appropriate medical help. This might mean taking the child to hospital or to a GP. Parents or carers should be informed but no discussion should take place about the cause of the injury.

In the context of sexual abuse, if sexual abuse is disclosed to a teacher then it is important for them to acknowledge to the child how painful it must have been to disclose this information but also to recognise that the process of investigation may be slower than that in physical abuse and that there needs to be more time to collate and evaluate information. Local authorities have been criticised, as in the Cleveland and Orkneys inquiries, when they have acted precipitately in the context of child sexual abuse.

Once the referral has been passed to social services, the social services department will allocate the case immediately to a social worker experienced in child protection and who will be supervised by a senior member of social services staff. An investigation will immediately be initiated, a medical examination requested and contact and discussion with the police will take place. Local authorities have joint working arrangements with the police and many have trained together and agreed protocol for child protection cases.

The investigative process may prove to be very difficult for teachers and support staff with particular reference to the suspected perpetrator, especially if that person is the parent or carer of the child and if there are other children of the same family at the school.

Where children are thought to be in imminent danger they may be removed from home on an Emergency Protection Order. It is very important that confidentiality is maintained for the sake of the child, their siblings and parent or carer and that staff have adequate support from senior staff at this difficult time.

The methods of working together will ensure that strategies are made between all the professionals involved in order to minimise any acrimony between parents and school staff. School social workers, education welfare officers and educational psychologists can provide excellent support and debriefing to staff at this time, which often leads to profound emotional distress for the injured child, for their siblings, and for parents or carers.

During the investigative process the social worker will probably involve the police, other professionals, parents or carers and the child and will then set up the child protection case conference. It is usual that all professionals involved in the situation together with parents or carers, and the child, where they are of a sufficient age to understand, will be involved in the case conference. Your own particular authority's protocol will be in the area child protection committee's guidelines and again it is important that these are read and followed.

The investigation process

There are many ways of investigating reported concerns about children. It would depend on the type of concern and what information is available. Most reported concerns are investigated within twenty-four hours of receiving the report and often within hours.

The social worker or their manager will check the following:

1. Whether the child is already known to the social services department and if so, what information is available. It is likely that school staff will already know whether children are of concern to the social services department.
2. Whether the child is on the area child protection register and if so under what category.
3. Who the general practitioner is. If this is known there is a possibility of contact with the GP to get information on their knowledge and experience of the child and their family.
4. Discussion with the head of the school or school child protection co-ordinator about the knowledge that they have.
5. Contact with any other professional person who may be able to give further information.

It should be noted that these investigations are carried out in the strictest of confidence.

The child protection case conference

It is the duty of the local authority social services department to initiate a case conference where there is serious concern that a child may have been abused or is in danger of abuse. All professionals who know the child or have a contribution to make will be asked to attend the case conference or to send a report. Class teachers will, therefore, be involved.

Parents or carers will be invited to the case conference with a solicitor or friend. Most local authorities now involve parents or carers in the entire case conference. Children will also be invited if they are of a significant age to understand the proceedings.

The child protection conference is an essential stage in joint work in individual cases and provides the prime forum for professionals, the family and the child, where appropriate, to share information and concerns, analyse levels of risks to the child or children and make recommendations for future action. It is not a forum for a formal decision that a person has abused a child this is a criminal offence and will be investigated by the police.

The prime tasks of the child protection case conference

1. To establish the facts about the circumstances giving rise to the concern;
2. To decide if there are grounds for concern;
3. To identify sources and level of risk;
4. To decide protective or other action in relation to the child and any others.

Decisions of the child protection conference

The child protection case conference will make decisions regarding the future of the child and their care.

1. Whether to place a child's name or family's name on the Child Protection Register;
2. Whether to de-register a family as in the review process;
3. If the child/children are registered, who will be the keyworker in the family;
4. What will be the child protection plan.

The keyworker will usually be the social worker who works for the local authority social services. They, along with their line manager, will form a core group of professional people who will regularly meet to discuss the progress of the child and their family or carers. The keyworker will therefore have a lot of contact with education staff and the person who has responsibility for the child in school.

The keyworker will also work in partnership with parents, carers and the child, to look at how best their needs for future help can be met.

In line with the 1989 Children Act, local authorities will be expected to work in partnership with parents; however, in cases of severe abuse it may be necessary for the child to leave the family home and be accommodated in a foster family or with relatives. In cases of serious abuse it may also be necessary for the abuser to leave home in order that the child can remain in their family. This may mean seeking a court order to achieve this.

In this entire process the teacher will be a key person in the core group and will be involved in the planning and therapeutic process of helping children and their families or carers come to terms with the abuse that has occurred and in helping to prevent abuse occurring again.

Keeping records in school

Information on children who are placed on a child protection register is routinely passed to schools together with a copy of the child protection plan formulated at the child protection case conference. All staff need to be aware of children who require careful vigilance and what help is being provided for them under the plan.

Careful records will need to be kept which can be made available when the child is reviewed. Child protection information on a child must be kept in separate files as the information is strictly confidential and should only be disclosed on a 'need to know' basis. Teachers need to know when a child is at risk and what the plan is, but may not need to know all the confidential details. Information should be kept up to date, in chronological order and in a form that is easily accessible. All this information should be kept by the headteacher or school child protection co-ordinator with contingency plans for when they are not at school.

Teachers with regular contact with the child may find it useful to keep a diary and jot down notes for their own use about the child from day to day. This will be a most useful reflective tool when it comes to the reviewing process. If a diary is used it should be kept in a safe place and should only be used as a record for that teacher.

The prevention of abuse in educational establishments

The joint HMSO, Department of Health, Department of Education and Science *Working Together under the Children Act 1989* clearly states that the National Curriculum Council has advised that children aged five years and above should begin to develop skills and practice which will help them to maintain personal safety. It has also identified family life, sex and safety education as three key components of education and has included family life education as a key topic in its advice to schools on education for citizenship.

There are a number of publications relating to health education and the development of a personal and social education curriculum already available in schools, both of which address issues of children being safe and of child protection issues. Some schools will be involved in inter disciplinary training around issues of child protection, others may depend totally on reading relevant publications and on information and advice they gain from other professional colleagues.

Child protection issues and sexual abuse

To be touched sexually by an adult when you are a child is sexual abuse. Child sexual abuse is committed in every class, religion, culture, race, and is more often than not committed by someone the child loves. The child is often left in isolation with dark, lonely secrets that they are afraid to tell. They become threatened by the perpetrator, violated and guilty. Their confusion strips them of their childhood innocence. The child will feel betrayed, vulnerable and have their trust and love of the perpetrator shattered. They will find it difficult to tell anyone that abuse has occurred and will not know how to say "no". Many adult survivors of childhood sexual abuse are left with a legacy of shame, guilt, anger and isolation, because they have been unable to speak about their experiences. Many of them talk about the hope that they had of confiding in a member of their school staff but always felt that they were unable to do so because of the high shame and horror they felt.

Signs of abuse in children

Teachers and support staff should be aware of signs which may be physical or behavioural in children who have been abused.

1. Unwillingness to undress for sports and games
2. Avoidance of physical contact
3. A frozen appearance
4. Unwillingness to return home

5. Truancy
6. Knowledge of or interest in sexual acts inappropriate for the child's age
7. Lack of concentration
8 Eating disorders
9. Constant anxiety
10. Sudden mood swings
11. Crying without reason
12. Acting out sexual behaviour
13. Excessive masturbation

Other signs in older children

In older children there may be other signs, such as:

1. Depression
2. Secretive behaviour
3. Suicidal thoughts
4. Low self esteem
5. Use of alcohol or drugs
6. Self mutilation.

This is not an exhaustive list but may help as triggers for staff in education establishments. It should also be used with caution as some of these symptoms may be indicative of other childhood and teenage distress.

If a child discloses sexual abuse to a teacher it means that they have a trusting relationship with that member of staff and at all costs that relationship must not be broken. It is therefore imperative that the staff member does not express shock or disbelief. It is highly unlikely that the child would be fabricating a story and they will have taken a long time to get to the point of disclosure.

The listening teacher or staff member must let the child know they can confide but also must help them to understand that they will need to share the information with other professionals to keep the child safe and in order that the disclosure can be dealt with and investigated appropriately.

It is important to remember that this process might take some time, but unlike physical abuse, sexual abuse has probably been occurring for a long time and thus the child is unlikely to be in imminent danger unless the perpetrator becomes aware of the disclosure. It is also necessary to remember that the abused child above all wants the abuse to stop and that often the abuse is happening between the child and someone whom they love. They will therefore not want life to be disrupted or the abuser necessarily punished.

Unfortunately for the child, once a disclosure has been made, it will be impossible for this to happen and to some degree it will cause further deprivation to the child. Much understanding and care is needed by the staff member when dealing with the child during the ordeal which surrounds disclosure and the subsequent consequences.

How abused children feel

As mentioned earlier in the chapter, a child who has suffered abuse will experience profound feelings which will distort their view on the world. They may include the following emotions.

Anger and resentment

The parental caring role has been abused, therefore the child feels anger towards the abuser. Conflict arises because the abuser may also be someone they love, especially if the abuser is a parent. There may be resentment because that parent has failed to protect the child.

Grief

The child grieves for the loss of the close bonded relationship between parent and child. Even if that bond has never been properly established, the child will grieve that it does not exist.

Confusion

Abusers confuse roles within families, often singling out a particular child whom they will abuse. This abuse frequently involves lying to the child, bribing them, threatening them, and treating them as an adult in some interactions and as a victim in others. It is a total abuse of the caring parental role and leads to emotional confusion in the child.

Betrayal

Children feel their love has been betrayed and this makes them doubt all relationships and suspicious of genuine offers of love and friendship. Typically such children will withdraw from many interactions as a form of emotional defence.

Self loathing

To maintain secrecy adults who abuse children have frequently encouraged children to share the blame for their actions. Children may well have felt sensual pleasure from some abuse which reinforces their feelings of guilt. The child will have a low self esteem and a strong dislike of themselves and their actions. They, therefore, become increasingly isolated from those around them.

Conclusion

Child abuse is one of the most emotive situations that staff in educational establishments will ever have to deal with and which will challenge all their own values. It is vitally important that the child's needs are put above all others and the practices already used in schools are adhered to in working in partnership with parents.

Children who have been abused will have demanding and changing needs. They may require individual therapy, family therapy or be part of a group run in schools for stressed children. Chapter 12 on groupwork gives information on the nature of groups in school, their management and how they can effectively help some children, who have been abused.

It is essential to take account of the importance of working together with other agencies and maintaining trust, both in the field of prevention, monitoring and therapy for children. Only by maintaining a good level of interagency co-operation and support can we hope that less children will be abused by their families or by their carers in the future.

References

Child abuse: a study of Inquiry Reports 1980-1989. HMSO 1991
Working together under The Children Act 1989. HMSO 1991
Elliott M 1988 *Keeping safe.* Hodder & Stoughton
Freeman L 1982 *It's my body: a book to teach young children how to resist uncomfortable touch.* Parenting Press Inc. USA
Jones D N 1987 *Understanding child abuse* 2nd edn. Macmillan

Lennit R, Crane B 1986 *It's OK to say no.* Thorsons (This book shows how children can protect themselves against sexual abuse by people they know as well as strangers)

Video
Kids can say no. A British made video produced by Rolf Harris and suitable for use in working with young school age children. Available from:
CFL Vision, Chalfont Grove, Gerrards Cross, Bucks.

Resource groups and organisations

Childline   24 hour free telephone counselling and advice for children who fear abuse or are in trouble.
              Tel 0800 1111
Kidscape   A national campaign aimed to introduce child sexual assault programmes into schools. Its primary object is to enable professionals to acquire the skills and techniques necessary to talk to children about good sense defence.
              Kidscape, 82 Brook Street, London, W1U 1YG. Tel 071-493 9845
National Society for the Prevention of Cruelty to Children (NSPCC)
              Headquarters, 67 Saffron Hill, London, EC1N 8RS. Tel 071-242 1626
              NSPCC Child Protection Helpline: 0800 800 500.

Wonder why you love me
I'm a world apart from your heart
You're so many skies above me
And you're a bloody tart.

I have no eyes for people
cause I'm a rocking rolling casual
strolling man.

Marriage is a killer
the end of many lives
my poor old heart is broken
smashed by twenty wives

Children cry for mummy
I think they cry everyday
So I take them back to
mummy, didn't want them anyway.

John Green

2   Divorce, separation and remarriage

Introduction

One in eight children are likely to experience divorce by the age of ten, and one in five by the age of sixteen. During the difficult stages which are involved in marital breakdown, society can often expect teachers to take over some of the responsibility for dealing with the stressed child. These notes are intended to share what is known about children's needs at this difficult time to enable teachers to have a better understanding of the problems and to guide their interactions with the children they teach. However, it is not our intention to suggest that they should become 'therapists' or to suggest that dealing with childhood stress is exclusively their responsibility.

The stresses experienced by families during a marital breakdown will inevitably spill over into performance in school and, as at any one time between three and five children in a mainstream class are likely to be involved, the issues raised will hopefully provide useful insight for all teachers and not just those with direct pastoral responsibilities.

Research indicates that divorce is a process which extends over a period of years and causes multiple stresses for children. Even when parents finally separate or divorce, children are likely to take between two and five years to adjust to their new situation.

Separating parents need to confirm their disengagement by alienating themselves from their partners. This can be very distressing for children who love both parents and have to witness rows or angry silences and who are subjected to one parent, or possibly both parents, justifying their actions to them, often in adult terms. It is known that children are unlikely to have reached a level of thinking which will allow them to understand what is happening from an adult perspective.

Marital break-up has a profound effect on children. Research suggests that it is not what children want, however difficult the parental relationship has become. Many children would prefer their parents to stay together and even after divorce or remarriage fantasize about a reunion. What they go through is akin to a bereavement and mourning process.

A child's self-esteem and sense of self worth is generated from a feeling of being part of an inherited identity which has come from both their parents. Familial traits are often commented on by friends and relatives and these attributes become part of the child's personal identity. During marital break-up and beyond, the criticisms which parents hurl at one another may leave a child feeling that part of their own identity is also bad and worthless. Frequently children experience a dramatic loss of self-esteem during separation and divorce. This can cause them to become very withdrawn and isolated, doubting their own value and ability. Alternatively, they can become excessively attention-seeking, desperate for adult approval. Both types of behaviour should be seen as a warning signal that the child will need help and support to rebuild their confidence in their own individual identity and worth.

As we are talking about between three and five children in any group of twenty, most teachers will be faced, at times, with children who are in the process of a major emotional trauma. It may take years for children to work through and come to terms with the issues involved. It is most important that people do not underestimate the stresses that children experience. Marital breakdown has a series of stages, each of which is likely to have a significant impact on children.

Avis Brenner in her book *Helping Children Cope with Stress* outlined the stages that children are likely to experience in some detail. We will now address some of the points she raises.

Stage one – the troubled marriage

The child's perception of the problems will depend on their age. Despite increased hostility between the parents, young children tend not to be aware of the tensions. School-aged children will notice the animosity between parents but their response will depend on how parents conduct themselves.

Some children will be witnessing physical or psychological aggression between the parents and may feel very frightened that someone will get hurt. This is also the stage when there can be a conspiracy of silence with parents reluctant to admit, even to themselves, that their marriage is running into serious difficulties.

Some children may try to create crises, to break this silence or to deflect attention away from the hostilities. Some copy parents' loud, irritable behaviour, some withdraw and others get drawn into taking sides in the marital war.

Changes in the child's behaviour can often alert a teacher to the fact that all is not well at home and the child may need an opportunity to talk through their worries with a trusted adult. They could also express their feelings through art, drama or creative writing.

It will be important that the trusted adult keeps any discussions with the child confidential, resisting the temptation to get involved in the dispute themselves by raising issues with parents, although they may want to mention observed behavioural changes to parents and share general school-centred concerns. Any disclosures of abuse, however, would of course need to be dealt with according to existing education and social services guidelines.

Stage two – separation(s)

There may be one or more trial separations at this stage. Very young children find this bewildering as each separation can seem to be final. They may regress developmentally and develop separation anxieties.

Contact with the absent parent can be fraught with problems. Unusual circumstances, for instance zoo visits, meeting in McDonalds, and so on, and hostile parental interactions at either end of the visit, combined with a reinforcement of the separation or loss as the visit ends, can all heighten the tensions.

Through this stage, children are trying to minimise the hostilities between their parents in the hope of reuniting them. Both parents are likely to be very angry and depressed themselves and are therefore unlikely to be able to give much emotional support to the children, which clearly increases their sense of loss.

Routines and roles at home may change and while there is a lot of coming and going, it may be difficult for children to adapt to the constant changes. In our experience, this time of apparent uncertainty tends to be extremely stressful for children and can often be reflected in a peak of behavioural problems.

What children need most at this stage is clear information about the future. However, as even parents are unlikely to have this worked out, it is difficult to help them. Teachers, if they are aware of what is happening, can work hard to keep a familiar and supportive environment going at school, being aware that children may be particularly distressed by any unfamiliar routines or changes of staff.

Stage three – transition and legal steps

At this stage, parents become engrossed in sorting out the practical details of life and they may unwittingly neglect their children, both physically and emotionally.

Many young children may regress to earlier behaviour patterns which makes them more dependent and demanding. Sleep disturbances, aggression and difficulties in enjoying play are also common.

Six to eight year olds experience a tremendous sense of loss for the parent who leaves. They may now become moderately depressed for some time. Clearly, this will affect their ability to learn in school and to maintain friendships.

As well as being depressed, nine to twelve year olds are likely to feel angry and are more prone to expressing their feelings directly. They may be forced to confront their parents' sexuality at a time when they are just beginning to experience these feelings themselves. Many children find this confusing or even distasteful.

At this stage, there are two things children need most. Firstly, they need the opportunity for clear discussion and explanation about what is happening with both parents. Secondly, they need to know that there will be regular contact with their absent parent. If this is not going to be the case they need to understand why this decision has been taken.

Clearly, there is little that teachers can do to facilitate this process unless they are asked for advice by parents. Yet again, teachers will need to be aware of the possible stress reactions in their pupils. Schools and teachers may be one of the few things in a child's life to remain constant throughout this difficult period. Whilst making certain allowances, it will also be important to at least try to maintain standards of achievement and behaviour.

Some children will see school as a haven away from home problems and in this case, they will not seek or welcome discussions of the difficulties at home. In each case the teacher will need to be guided by what seems to work best for a particular child or situation.

Whilst teachers may now find themselves dealing with only one parent, ideally reports on children's progress should be available to both parents, and both parents should have an opportunity to discuss with school staff any difficulties that arise in school. Where couples find it difficult to meet and talk about their children amicably together, separate meetings will need to be arranged.

Stage four – divorce and aftermath

A number of factors will come into play in the aftermath of the divorce. Parents are likely to have less time for their children as both partners often now have to work to support the two households; the mother may have to move to less desirable accommodation and may lose her social status as a consequence of the divorce. There will be less money to spend on everything and a period of financial adjustment will be necessary. Where a house move has resulted in a new neighbourhood or school, children will have to adjust to the new peer group, teachers, and so on. There may be new adult partners and possibly new step-siblings. Loss of extended family, especially relatives of the absent parent, may be particularly distressing if they were close and much loved.

Children often have difficulty discussing these changes with peers, tending to be defensive in relationships, guarding their feelings against further pain. There may be worry about parents' well being, or about getting involved in having to act as messengers and spies between warring parents. They may have to take on more household responsibility or they may be stressed by feeling guilty about still caring for the 'bad' parent. They may experience an identity crisis if previously they identified closely with the absent parent, as described earlier.

Children may need a day or two off school to adjust to the new home situation but if parents sanction a longer absence, it can lead to withdrawal into depression with increasing inability to face the world. The child's recovery will inevitably involve periods of going and doing something which takes their mind off immediate problems. Going to school regularly and having to conform to school routine can, in this way, be very therapeutic.

The first year

The whole of this time can also be one of great difficulty for the child. A sense of loneliness, sadness and difficulties concentrating at school, all contribute to heightened emotionality which makes relating to others and coping with schoolwork problematic.

Teachers need to affirm the pain that children experience and to be helpful and supportive when tiredness, absences, late arriving or lack of kit signal a chaotic time at home. Often children will show distress by being pre-occupied in class, not completing assignments or by being argumentative and even aggressive with peers. Teachers can help them to regain their balance by requiring the same standards of them as of the rest of the class, listening to their concerns rather than smothering them with sympathy, and stepping back from making judgements about what is happening at home. Encouraging children to develop hobbies and interests which will divert attention away from their problems, will also help.

Long-term issues

Of the one in five children affected by divorce by the age of sixteen, up to half will have lost contact with the non-custodial parent (usually the father) by the end of the first year. The decision to discontinue contact is often made in the belief that the child will 'get over it' and that it will be better for the child. However, the long-term prognosis for children of divorced parents, research indicates, is that those who never see their non-custodial parent are the least well adjusted both at school and at home.

Where joint custody is arranged, splitting time between two households can also cause problems. Remarriage and the creation of step-families introduce yet more issues. Each partner in the new marriage brings their own expectations and ideas about family life to the partnership and step-siblings may be at very different development stages; one may be approaching adulthood whilst the step-family prepares for the birth of a new baby for example. Equally, some children find themselves sharing attention, and perhaps toys, clothes and a bedroom, with a step-sibling of the same age. Families require time to build new roles and routines in relation to the parent interactions as well as parent/child interactions. Whilst this process is taking place, children can yet again experience stress and tension.

One study found that five years after divorce, 37 per cent of children interviewed were still moderately to severely depressed. As Brenner says, 'It is important to recognise that the years of tension building up to the divorce and the two to five years of adjustment which follow can occupy a large fraction or even the totality of youngsters' childhood'.

Table 1.   Children's reaction to marital breakdown according to age

Age	Thoughts	Some Typical Responses Feelings	Behaviour
Pre-school (up to 6 years old)	Thought processes are still at a very egocentric and concrete level. They tend to measure love by physical proximity. Therefore they think that they have caused Mummy or Daddy to go away and illogically but sensibly presume that it must have been because of something wrong with them. They cannot understand, and therefore remember, adult explanations.	Incomprehension, guilty for causing divorce, afraid, bewildered, frustrated. Fearful of losing remaining parents. Worried and jealous that the absent parent may have found a 'better' child to love.	Regression to earlier behaviours. Separation anxiety. Sleep disturbances. Loss of enjoyment in play activities. Aggressive play. Possibly the cause of a slow start at school.
5–8 year olds	Still egocentric, but more aware of parental conflict. Now believe that their behaviour caused the fights between parents, leading to marital breakup. This logic leads them to believe that they can do something which will bring about a reconciliation. They think that the length and frequency of visits from the absent parent are dependent on their behaviour during visits. Failure will result in the missing parent finding another child to love.	Frightened. Disorganised. Grieving. Reconciliation fantasies. Inhibits aggression towards father but angry towards mother. Loyalty conflicts. Worrying about seeing enough of the absent parent.	Boys take out aggressive feelings on objects rather than on peers. Girls become closer to mother. But 4 to 10 years after divorce, delayed reactions may be:- poor concentration, underachievement, aggressive and disruptive behaviour, particularly in boys. Boys cope with remarriage better than girls.
9–12 year olds	Beginning to develop a better understanding of other people's points of view. Have now realised that adults can change and no longer be in love; but do not understand why this happens. They believe that things could be put right if parents tried hard enough. They feel that parents are being selfish if they can't do this. 'Civilised' separations cause confusion – if parents seem to be amicable, why can't they live together? Because child and adult perceptions of a situation may be so discrepant, both sides can have great difficulty in communicating with and understanding each other.	Loyalty conflicts and ambivalence about parents. Identity problems. Anger. Worthlessness. Embarrassment about parents' sexuality. Possibly desire to keep the divorce a secret. Fear of being different. May feel responsible for welfare of parents and younger siblings.	May behave excessively well in the belief that this will reunite parents. May create crises to divert parental hostilities or to force parents to talk to one another. May get drawn into marital war. Reduced attention to schoolwork. Psychosomatic illnesses. Later adolescent delinquency. In girls increased adolescent anti-social behaviour, early sexual activity, seek male attention. Depression.
Adolescents	Concern about parents' motives. Anxious about own ability for lasting marriage.	Withdrawal from parents. Mourning of marriage. Depressed. Angry. Conflicting loyalties. Resentment over any loss of income and consequent change of lifestyle. Embarrassed or threatened by having to acknowledge parents as sexual beings. May feel responsible for well-being of parents and younger siblings – or resentment at being expected to take on more family responsibilities. Troubling memories of parental violence or hostility often haunt adolescents.	Regression or pseudo maturity. Angry outbursts. Withdrawal. Depressed behaviour. More likely than younger age group to show direct feelings of hostility and resentment. Movement towards independence may be halted or accelerated.

Classroom management

Be alert to changes in behaviour. A sudden deterioration in work output or a spate or naughtiness can be an early signal that there are problems at home. Equally, the child who is withdrawn and finding it difficult to join in with class activities or games in the playground may be signalling distress.

If you routinely have an opportunity to meet with a parent or parents you might mention the changes you have noticed to them and ask if they are aware of similar changes at home, or whether there is anything that has happened or is happening that could be causing the child to be showing signs of distress. Parents sometimes underestimate the effect that the loss of a friend, a pet or even a member of their extended family, can have on a child, and such misunderstandings can then be cleared up and the problem dealt with appropriately. Equally, such initial enquiries can give the teacher an early warning that the child is in for some troubled times ahead and so can be well prepared to offer support if needed. Understandably, parents are often reluctant to discuss marital problems with anyone outside the family. If parents insist that all is well, little will be gained by pressing them further although your original intuitions may prove to be correct.

There are strong conventions in our society which are reinforced in the media about how families are supposed to operate. When children feel that their family circumstances are outside such norms they feel isolated and have difficulty relating to their peers.

Although children may become very attention-seeking as a result of the insecurity caused by marital disharmony, few would welcome direct questions about home. It is often better to be available as a reassuring listener when needed. Children need to have a balance of support strategies on offer to them when they are coping with stress. Activities are the most useful way of offering support as they are 'safer', leaving children feeling more directly in control of their level of involvement.

Broadly speaking there are four types of support activities which can be incorporated into the normal curriculum.

Activities which enable or facilitate 'working through the problem'

These will include stories, discussions and TV programmes which address the issues around separation and divorce, helping the whole class to sort out their attitudes and feelings, without focusing directly on the troubled child. Discussions can help children to realise that they are not alone and that others face similar problems. Children may also want to make use of diaries, creative writing or paintings and drawings to comment upon or sort out their understanding of what is happening to them.

Those who have difficulty expressing themselves on paper may use play activities or, for older children, drama to work through situations. Sometimes children will feel safer talking about their experiences and feelings if they can project them on to a doll or puppet. 'Teddy's unhappy today, his mummy's cross with him and he doesn't know why'. For younger children time in the Wendy House is often used in this way. Older children can also benefit from such activities, but in their case the tasks may need to be more contrived.

When, as a teacher, you are aware that a child's family are experiencing problems, it can be helpful to establish a member of staff who the child would feel comfortable going to if they had a problem. That person could then arrange the easiest way to be contacted if needed, sometimes even setting aside a regular time (for instance, ten minutes Tuesday lunchtime) to check that all is well. This will help the child feel that their difficulties are recognised, and can be a particularly helpful strategy for the child who is very attention-seeking as it gives the one-to-one attention, whilst focusing it on a time which fits in with other demands on the teacher. In research studies children report that talking to others who have had similar experiences is helpful, as is talking to older siblings or informed adults about what is likely to happen in the future.

Active distractions

Some activities will helpfully take the child's mind away from immediate problems. The general routine of school work will fall into this category, and helping the child keep up their level of attainment where possible can be useful in this way.

Sporting activities and hobbies can usefully help the child to develop a wider social network spilling over into out-of-school hours. This may help to take pressure off fraught home situations for older children. Also, the physical energy expended during sporting activities enables the body to get rid of waste products which build up in tissues as a result of the hormonal response to stressful situations.

Emotional expression

Activities which give children opportunities for emotional expression need not relate directly to their problems. So, although some children may want to express their feelings through art work, creative writing or poetry, they will equally benefit from activities which allow for emotional expression for its own sake. Playing a musical instrument, crying during a sad film, laughing at a comedy or shouting at a football match will all encourage the release of pent-up emotions and feelings.

Heightened emotionality sometimes causes worry in school, especially when it is noticed in boys, but it is a normal response to stressful situations and will pass in time. Tearfulness or aggression should be dealt with in a calm, matter-of-fact way which will reassure the child.

Nurturing and confidence building

As we have described earlier, many of the things that happen during a matrimonial breakdown have a very damaging effect on a child's self-esteem. Even children who appear to have gone through the trauma relatively unscathed will undoubtedly have had their confidence severely shaken. They need to understand that they are individuals in their own right and that they are valued as such. Often the stresses at home have led them into being quarrelsome and aggressive at school, socially isolated and unpopular. This can lead to a vicious circle of negative feedback with the child feeling trapped and helpless to change the situation whilst being desperately unhappy about how badly they are behaving. They need clear messages which confirm their value as an individual from the adults around them to help them through this. Their behaviour may be unacceptable, but they as an individual are liked, valued and wanted.

There are many published activities which can be used to build self-confidence which will benefit all pupils and not just those who are experiencing trauma. One particularly good source of ideas in this area is the Kingston Friends Workshop Group's book *Ways and Means*, as these activities fit so well with national curriculum requirements and are adaptable to any age.

Summary

1. Children signal distress through their behaviour

2. Check with parents if you observe worrying changes in children
3. Children in stressful circumstances feel very isolated
4. Try to be a good listener and to make time available for the child to talk to you
5. Make sure you offer a range of support activities to cater for varying needs.

Listening to and counselling children

If children seem to want to talk about what is happening, adopting the stance of sympathetic listener is probably the most generally helpful approach. The following points may also be relevant:

(a) Try to recognise and keep in check any feelings and prejudices you may have about marital breakdown.

(b) Children and families usually find their own solutions to crises eventually and should be allowed to do so. It is tempting to give lots of advice but it can prevent people from finding their own way through problems.

(c) Try not to criticise either parent, but allow the child to do so if they wish and accept their feelings or anger.

(d) In your desire to help children feel better, try to avoid leading them to expect unrealistic improvements of solutions to the situation, such as 'I'm sure daddy will be home soon'. A comment like 'Things will work out in the end' might be a useful, comforting phrase.

(e) Use simple words for emotions, for example, sad, cross, lonely, mixed-up, fed up.

(f) Primary aged children in particular may need reassurance that they are not the only family that this has happened to, given the picture of a nuclear family which is often portrayed by society and in the media.

(g) It is often helpful to encourage the child to think about whether there is a relative or friend of the family who could be a special friend during this time.

(h) If a child clams up, don't press the conversation further.

(i) You need to respect the child's confidentiality. However, you may feel that it is appropriate to let a few key members of staff know that all is not well. Equally, you may find the child's distress upsetting or emotionally draining and may need to discuss your own feelings or what to do next with a trusted colleague.

(j) Finally, although at times everything may seem very negative and stressful, it is important to remember that even the most difficult situations generally do change, develop and eventually resolve.

Practical support

There are a number of practical things to do which can be helpful. The child who is new to the school because of a move of house associated with marital separation will need extra help to settle in, become familiar with the school and feel welcome. It would be useful to ensure that one member of staff is given the specific responsibility for looking after the child's well-being in the early days. Children whose home lives seem chaotic whilst the adults focus on sorting out their lives, may need extra support and understanding as regards arriving at school at the right time, having the right equipment and so on. It may be difficult for them to concentrate on homework at home and they may welcome an opportunity to have access to a quiet room to do homework during the dinner time. If they miss some schooling, they will need help to catch up on missed lessons. Remember that money for such things as school uniform and school trips may be tight. Be sensitive towards children whose sleep patterns have been disturbed because they are upset or because of changed routines and circumstances at home.

Reference materials

It would be useful to keep some age-appropriate reading material around in the classroom or library that children could dip into if they so wish. Possibilities include:

Divorce and you – a leaflet produced by the Children's Society, 1988, Edward Rudolf House, Margery Street, London WC1 0JL
When parents split up by A Mitchell, 1986, Chambers
It's not the end of the world by J Blume, 1982, Heinemann Educational
It's not my life by R Leason, 1980, Collins

Helping children to cope with anger and despair

Children may display their anger and despair at marital break-up by being aggressive at school. Clearly, teachers will need to deal with this, especially when the safety of others is at risk. Equally, most children don't enjoy behaving badly, with the consequent disapproval and embarrassment at their own actions, so from this point of view also it is reasonable to help them to try and control their behaviour. In any methods which are used, the key factor is to remember that criticism of the child as a person will exacerbate the underlying emotional distress. Thus, an exclusively punitive approach of telling the child that they are naughty, bad, unkind etc. is to be avoided. The gist of the message needs to be that you like the child but dislike their behaviour. As is generally the case in dealing with any difficult behaviour, problems are likely to be minimalised by adopting a very quiet, calm, controlled and unemotional manner. Expressing disapproval of poor behaviour should also be linked with some discussion on ways to help the child behave better in the future.

Some pupils may be able to agree to remove themselves from a situation to a previously agreed place or to tell a particular adult if they feel in a mood which is likely to result in an aggressive act. In other cases, it may be possible for teachers to see trouble brewing and suggest quietly to the child that perhaps they should go off to a quiet place to calm down.

Another useful strategy could be getting the child to count to ten. When the child is calm and relaxed, they should be encouraged to practise counting slowly to ten, associating each number with a colour, an image or a smell which is pleasant. Children will need to rehearse this several times to familiarise themselves with the associations. Usually by the time they have run through the sequence, they will be feeling calm again. Alternatively, a nursery rhyme or a catchy tune with a few verses will have the same effect, for instance 'This old man....'

Clearly distraction or counselling techniques as outlined above are also worth exploring as a means of reducing aggressive behaviour. However, teachers should beware of giving long counselling sessions immediately after poor behaviour, as some children quickly learn that behaving badly is a good way of getting their teacher's undivided, sympathetic attention.

Referral to other agencies

Other agencies which might become involved in helping children and families deal with marital break-up include child guidance services, school psychological services, social services departments and Relate. Referral to another agency may be advisable if a child displays extreme and prolonged distress by either a depressive, withdrawn reaction or a hostile, acting out, behavioural reaction. Persistent and unlikely fantasies about the missing parent or parental reunion also suggest that specialist help would be useful. The services offered by these agencies may vary to some degree from area to area and it would be useful to get to know where these services are located, what they offer and their referral procedures. Referral to outside agencies would need to be discussed with the child's parents, except in cases of suspected abuse, in which case the procedures laid down by the social services department in conjunction with the local education authority should be followed.

References

Arnold L. E. 1990 *Childhood Stress*. John Wiley & Sons
Bowers S. Wells L 1987 Ways and means: an approach to problem solving.
   The handbook of Kingston Friends Workshop Group. Lexington Books
Brenner A 1984 *Helping children cope with stress*. Lexington Books

3 Depression in childhood and adolescence

Introduction

Childhood depression quite rightly has received increasing attention in the literature during the last forty years (Bowlby 1960, Seagull 1990, Kazdin 1989). There has been much confusion in this field with views ranging as far apart as the claim that children do not suffer from significant depression (Angold 1988) to the view that depression occurs as a specific illness in childhood and adolescence similar to that of adults. There is now a consensus of opinion that although different from adult depression, depression does exist as a major disease in childhood and may in many cases be a significant and underlying cause of various social and health-related difficulties.

Depression may exist in its own right or be associated quite significantly with aspects of behavioural difficulties associated with teenage pregnancy, substance abuse, eating disorders, suicide, serious accidents, violent crimes, and psychosomatic disorders.

The fact that depression as a clinical syndrome can be diagnosed in children, adolescents and adults does not mean that the manifestations of this disorder are identical in each phase of life. Childhood is a time of learning, developing and growing and discovering life's opportunities and challenges. Each developmental stage has a healthy pattern of functioning with associated normal characteristics. The presentation of depression in childhood and adolescence differs according to the age and the developmental level of the child (Kazdin 1989).

A wide variety of symptoms besides the obvious ones of sadness and a sense of misery may be present and these feelings may be associated with other types of disorders such as anorexia nervosa, conduct disorder, attention deficit, hyperactivity disorder, school phobia, somatic illness, the initial and important phases of psychosis in adolescence and obsessive and compulsive disorders.

The term depression can be referred to as a symptom or as an illness, (Kazdin 1989) or in the case of childhood and adolescence, as a syndrome of symptoms that go together. In its simplest form sadness as a presentation in depression is part of a larger set of problems that includes loss of interest in activities, a feeling of worthlessness and helplessness, associated sleep disturbances, changes in appetite, behavioural problems and psychosomatic complaints.

Depression in toddlers and infants

Physical or emotional neglect associated with a sense of emotional loss or separation from a loved person without appropriate substitute adequate care is a frequent cause of depression in toddlers and infants (Bowlby 1960, Seagull 1990).

The most characteristic symptoms of depression in this age group are associated with eating disturbances, with failure to gain weight, a significant development delay, a loss of already acquired achievement with associated regressive symptoms, sleep disturbance and a tendency to persistent illness. An important early indicator of depression is the marked behaviour association with abnormal separation anxiety, with clinging behaviour to parents or adults, particularly at night associated with nightmares or night terrors. Sometimes vague somatic complaints with no organic explanation are an initial presentation.

Under these conditions some children appear to be obedient, dependent and compliant but they are very clinging and sulky. There is a marked diminution of interaction between themselves and their siblings and with other adults, indicating quite significant underlying lack of security, anxiety and depression.

Depression of six to twelve year olds

Depression in young children of this age group is largely under-recognised and misunderstood by professionals and parents, even though estimates in the USA indicate that 10 per cent of the children suffer from some form of depression before age twelve, (Dolgan 1990).

This misunderstanding is partly due to the lack of ability for young children to express in words feelings which are important to them. They find it very difficult to accurately tell us about their inner feelings and will seldom come to you and say "I am feeling depressed" or "I am feeling helpless and hopeless".

Although they lack the ability to express in words their inner feelings, depressed effect is a condition *sine qua non* of the clinical diagnosis of depression. Children with moderate to severe depression look distinctly unhappy and sad and there is a flat emotional presentation. Smiles are fleeting and quickly replaced by a bland frozen look. The distinction between an unhappy and a 'depressed' child can be made in part by determining the duration of the child's downcast mood which is only short in the unhappy child. Information about the duration of mood change should be sought from multiple sources, including teachers, parents and child. These children describe themselves in negative terms, such as stupid or not popular, or admit that friends call them derogatory nicknames, which are all signs of low self-esteem. As they usually are sensitive about their self-esteem, they may try to hide the accompanying emotions. Depressed children disproportionately collect real or perceived rejections, which further lowers self-esteem. Feeling unloved and being used by others, is often associated with a sense of helplessness, hopelessness and a lack of confidence. They sense that everything is going wrong – whatever they try to do seems to be bad and the 'bad' always conquers the 'good' and this never seems to change. They don't have very much hope for improvement of feeling any better, neither do they see an outcome for their unhappy situation.

Enjoyment is an integral part of a child's life and a necessary component for learning, growing and playing. Depressed children are often unable to describe what they do for fun. Pleasure-evoking activities are perceived without any sense of anticipation or pleasure. Depressed children are apathetic and listless and not interested in activities which children of their own age find pleasurable, such as sports, hobbies and mixing with others. They resist opportunities to play or mix with other children. They may directly state that they have friends but that their friends do not like them. In play they repeatedly set themselves up to be rejected by others. Mildly depressed children may long for social relationships and turn to a dog or a cat for a substitute friend. More severely depressed children no longer seek friends. When the child has been able to socialise well prior to the onset of the depression these changes are even more strikingly observed.

Complaints of fatigue are common in depressed children. They report taking voluntary naps or feel 'tired' and do not want to participate in any activity. This feeling of exhaustion is not secondary to physical exertion, it occurs before or without activity. Once it is established that chronic fatigue is present we have to determine its duration or timing. Does it occur the same time every day, for instance when the school bus is arriving? Has it been present for one month or six months? Besides feeling tired, depressed children may sit in a slumped posture and stare at the floor, and are often seen as hypoactive. Their speech can be noticeably flat and expressionless, and slowed up, they answer questions in monosyllables.

Despite being tired, a large number of depressed children have difficulty in sleeping. Generally they are more aware of the sleep disturbance than the parents. They describe sleep problems with convincing accuracy. They need only to be asked: "Do you have trouble sleeping?" and then they immediately report difficulty in falling asleep, waking during the night, early morning waking and associated nightmares and terrors.

Not eating well brings parental disapproval, it is not surprising therefore that the child does not often talk about loss of appetite. Parents, however, report a disinterest in food and gradual weight loss in their depressed child.

As a reaction to the underlying depressive system and apart from the feelings we described earlier children develop different coping mechanisms; one of 'flight or escape', or 'fight or aggression' (Sanders-Woudstra 1986) (Pamela Keneally 1988). In the flight or escape scenario, poor school attendance with recurrent psychosomatic problems, running away from home or wandering aimlessly in the community, can often be associated with quite noticeable social withdrawal and lack of contact with peers and an aimless wandering away from problems. Difficult clinging behaviour which provokes parental irritability may indicate a retreat from the peer group and natural social activities and may often be associated with excessive comfort symptoms of indulgence in sweets, rhythmic rocking or even excessive masturbation.

The complex interaction between psychosomatic symptoms and depressive feelings often leads to difficulties in educational progress and poor school performance. The associated symptoms of poor concentration, lethargy, fatigue, lack of energy, lack of motivation, will certainly be picked up in school assessment and may be indicative of underlying depressive feelings affecting a child's school performance. School attendance may become a problem but the actual non-attendance itself as an indicator of depression may be covered by problems attributed to physical illness. Somatic complaints such as abdominal pain, headaches, chest pains without any obvious organic findings, can be an indication that the young person is somatising their problems. If this is not understood and picked up by parents and professionals this will often lead to poor school attendance.

In the fight scenario the symptoms of hyperactivity, agitation, acting out, provocative and aggressive behaviour attract a considerable amount of attention to the child. The child feels helpless and hopeless and basically feels that it doesn't matter what they do. Small thefts can lead to major episodes of delinquent behaviour which can include arson and quite worrying acts of physical aggression. The depressed child is, in this situation, effectively trying to drown their depressive mood, feelings and associated anxiety by deflecting attention from themselves with their aggressive and overactive behaviour.

There tends to be a difference in presentation between boys and girls. Boys tend to go in for the 'fight reaction' whilst girls tend to choose the 'flight reaction', but clearly the overall presentation will be strongly determined by the underlying personality of the child, their reactions to their peer group and the relationships the child has with teachers, parents and important family members.

All the signs we described earlier should be taken together as an indicator of the depressed child's underlying feelings, particularly when there is a noticeable change in mood, behaviour or function of the child. Change can often be dramatic particularly following important life events such as parental separation or death of a loved one. Close observation of the change enables one to see the variation in the child's pattern of previous behaviour and compare it with their current functioning.

No particular indicator is diagnostic of depression in a child but when a number of symptoms are clustered together, in association with important external life events affecting a child, then they must be taken seriously.

Depression in pre-puberty

Many children entering this stage of development have the ability to show a depressive mood and to talk about their feelings of depression or anxiety or suicidal ideation. The depressive feelings can, however, be masked by the 'fight' or 'flight' behaviour described in the pre-pubertal group.

Depression in adolescence

The assessment of depression in adolescence becomes easier because of the adolescent's ability to articulate their feelings and the increasing clarity of presentation of their mood state. They can provide an accurate account of how they are feeling and an adolescent may well say "I am feeling depressed". Peer group assessments of the adolescent's functioning are also an important indicator. They will often talk of their friends as being sad or depressed, they may worry about them and upon direct questioning of their peers one can ask them direct and important questions – do they smile often?, do they look sad or unhappy?

It is important to recognise that the feelings of sadness and of negativity are perfectly normal in adolescent development (Sanders-Woudstra). However, when these feelings are associated with strong elements of self-blame, worthlessness, self-depreciation and hopelessness then there is a very real likelihood of underlying depressive feelings. Many adolescents often feel quite impotent and unable to control or change their lives but a total sense of apathy, loss of interest of life and inability to obtain any sort of pleasure from the activity of organising themselves is an indication of underlying depression.

Physiological factors can be picked up, such as changes of appetite and sleep pattern with early or frequent wakening, difficulties in falling asleep or drowsiness and lack of concentration and attention. General physical retardation is often noticed together with elements of restlessness and heightened sense of irritability. One has to be particularly cautious of these adolescents since suicide is very common in those who are showing signs of restlessness and agitation.

An adolescent's membership of a peer group is vitally important to enable them to develop their identity and cope with the difficult transition from adolescence into adulthood. The peer group becomes a safe halfway house between the family and the adult world. The adolescent in transition is vulnerable just as the lobster is when it sheds its shell! (Dolto 1988) Someone who appears on the surface to be an exemplary school pupil to adults may be one who is left out of the peer group, who is in fact a loner and has to cope with a strong sense of loss and failure. Under such circumstances these adolescents are particularly vulnerable and carry a high risk of depression leading to a suicidal attempt (Gay, Armsden et al 1990).

The important reactive behaviour of adolescents sometimes leads to quite impulsive life-threatening behaviour. Adolescence is very much a time of mood swings with strong emotional reactions to immediate life events. The break up of a relationship with a boyfriend or girlfriend or a major row within the family situation can be interpreted by the adolescent as total rejection, leaving them with a sense of loss so great it may lead to depression and the associated risk of attempted suicide.

The whole area of risk taking behaviour in adolescence can be complicated by underlying feelings of depression and hopelessness, so much so that the adolescent feels that they might as well take a risk if they have 'nothing to lose'. Delinquent behaviour, aggression, drug abuse, sexual promiscuity, are all important risk taking activities. These can be seen at times as attention seeking or problem solving behaviour or they may even become morbid preoccupations as far as the adolescent is concerned. If the adolescent continues to have an inner sense of hopelessness and helplessness then there is a very great risk that they will not take the natural and necessary precautions to avoid this more obvious type of acting out behaviour leading to quite significant self-harm.

Knowing when to intervene in the process of assessment and diagnosis of depression in adolescents is a very complex process, since depression itself is not synonymous with sadness which is a perfectly normal expression in adolescence. Emotional lability and elements of loneliness, boredom and despondency again are to be expected and they are certainly very frequently used words by adolescents to describe how they feel, so too are fluctuations of mood; one moment they are buoyed up by their high spirits, the next moment they are cast down and feel totally isolated and withdraw from relationships. It is only when these patterns of behaviour begin to persist that one can specifically determine the underlying element of depression. A prolonged period of lack of interest, poor concentration, low physical and emotional activity, high levels of frustration must make parents and teachers cautious about an adolescent and their functioning since it can be the indication of an onset of depression or of a more serious psychotic episode which can be heralded by a period of depression. The evaluation of the duration and the pervasiveness of the symptoms therefore need very careful scrutiny. It is essential to use all the possible available resources of the family, the school and the community to bring together the best possible description of the pattern of the functioning of the adolescent over a period of time before making a clear diagnosis.

Attempted suicide

According to Kelly (1991) the attempted or completed suicide very often starts off as an alarm signal put out by the adolescent indicating their underlying feelings of helplessness and sadness and can be seen as a cry for help after many other attempts at communication have failed. Many adolescents feel that they are not understood and that their cries for help are not heard.

Most attempted suicides in adolescents are impulsive rather than planned acts. The availability of a means of suicide, such as drugs, in association with a depressive mood, can often lead to an impulsive desire to die or to get back at someone which can result in a fatal outcome.

There is an increasing awareness now of the underlying pattern of depression in adolescent attempted suicide and self-destructive behaviour. Suicide is the third most important cause of death in the adolescent age group in the USA after accidents and homicide. Boys tend to be more likely to complete suicide although adolescent girls tend to make more suicide attempts. Suicide itself does not always occur during the course of a depressive disorder but may occur in the course of events in other psychiatric disorders and as an impulsive reaction.

A quite separate presentation of depression in adolescence can occur in bipolar or unipolar depressive disorders with a strong familial background. Depression in adolescence can be the first manifestation of a bipolar disorder. In such circumstances the period of depression may often be followed by periods of hypomania or mania with the manic symptoms presenting as hyperactivity, insomnia, restlessness, irritability, talkativeness, associated with grandiose delusions of intelligence, power or attractiveness and hypersexuality. Delusions of persecution and flights of ideas are also found in this age group. There is often a strong family history of affective disorder and although the individual episodes of depression are responsive to medication there can be a recurrence of the depressive disorder or of the bipolar presentation with manic episodes.

Risk factors associated with the development of depression

Vulnerability

Some children are more vulnerable than others and the importance of individual differences must be stressed. The presentation of depressive symptoms often comes about through a combination of stress factors affecting an already vulnerable young person. If the stress factors are greater than the child's ability to tolerate stress because of important criteria such as age, previous experience, family stress, lack of social support, then depressive feelings may develop and become all pervasive.

In some young people quite minor factors can precipitate stress, such as the physical illness of a sibling, anticipation of change, loss of friendship or failure of some anticipated goal.

The loss of a loved one

The ability of a young person to tolerate the threatened separation or loss of an important adult is influenced by many factors including the quality of attachment that the young person has to the adult. The abruptness of separation and whether or not there has been any preparation prior to it and the presence or absence of support systems available to them are significant factors. Parental death is a major cause of childhood depression and a depressive reaction is to be expected in situations of sudden death. Matrimonial situations leaving the child with one parent are often experienced by the child as a loss, particularly if problems of contact or access arise due to the continuing conflict between the parents.

When a parent is depressed or has problems of alcoholism they are often not emotionally available to their child. There is an important loss of 'involvement with the child' which can be regarded as parental loss. There is often a considerable amount of family tension and conflict and associated disorganisation and loss of structure which lead to ineffective parenting in these households. Depressive parents frequently have quite unrealistic expectations towards their children and will place a considerable amount of responsibility on the children for their own physical and psychological well-being, and even encourage a feeling that they can be dependent upon their own children for emotional support, care and attention.

Associated frequent hospitalisations for depression or alcoholism with changing care givers provides a disruption in the life of the child which is significant and can leave the child feeling vulnerable.

Living with depressive parents can be an adverse model of 'reaction to stress' for a child. There is a considerable risk that the children may react to stress in a similar fashion.

Life-threatening illness, chronic illness and frequent hospitalisations

When illness occurs within the family system, particularly if it is of a chronic nature, many family members get caught up in the medical and nursing aura surrounding the illness and healthy children can very easily feel totally forgotten, constantly having to cope with the threat of death of a loved one at a time when they are effectively being ignored as far as their own emotional feelings are concerned. Sometimes the healthy siblings can over-identify with their sick brother, sister or parent and can produce either an angry response, in the sense that they find it difficult to understand why their sibling is ill, or a depressive one where they get a sense of desperation and impending loss. Children can get caught up in the family's guilt feeling about the sick family member. They can blame themselves for being the cause of the illness or for not being ill themselves – 'Why him and not me?'

In familial illness like diabetes or fibrocystic disease, they may experience strong personal anxiety about being affected themselves.

Child physical and sexual abuse and neglect

Neglect and abuse frequently leave children feeling totally helpless, hopeless and worthless. Depression itself is intertwined with the maltreatment of children in complex ways. With physical abuse it is often a reflection of the feeling of not being wanted or loved which reinforces a sense of low self-esteem and rejection. When the abuse is associated with parental depression or alcoholism this adds an additional burden for the vulnerable child (Allan 1989 and Eliott 1990).

Scapegoating

Vulnerability may come from a process of scapegoating within the family or peer group setting. Intense feelings of depression and despair can be experienced by children who are bullied, teased and picked on. These feelings only go to further emphasise to the young person that they really are quite helpless and worthless and friendless individuals. Quite often successful suicidal attempts appear to be the end product of a long pattern of teasing, provocation and abuse which has gone on undetected and is seen by the young person as being intolerable.

Genetic factors associated with depression

There has been a recent increased interest in the genetics of affective disorders in childhood and adolescence.

A considerable amount of research has been done in the field of genetics on adult depression but one has to be very cautious about extrapolating findings from the adult age group to that of childhood or adolescence. In many ways the presentation and cause of childhood depression is different from that of adult depression.

Individuals who have developed an early onset (before the age of twenty) of serious bi and unipolar affective disorders are more likely to have a strong genetic component to these disorders.

Parents who have early onset affective disorders are more likely to have children presenting serious depression before the age of fifteen.

Some studies note that children may demonstrate minor symptoms of depression years before the full-blown bipolar disorders appear after puberty. The familial loading for major affective disorder in first degree relatives seems to be significantly higher when the bipolar disorder in the parent is preceded by symptoms before the age of twelve (early symptoms may include hyperactivity, conduct disorder, psychosomatic disorder).

Considerable care needs to be taken when trying to draw conclusions from familial patterns of presentation since it is possible to indicate that either genetic or environmental influences or both are affecting the presentation of the symptoms in the young person.

What to do

Prevention

The average child or adolescent spends a large part of their life in school, the school environment therefore creates a unique environment to provide a strong preventative influence on the young person. The emotional and physical availability of teachers, as sensitive and aware adults, is vitally important where children are at risk. Those made vulnerable by parental loss, somatic illness or threatened danger can pick up a sense of security from the teacher, who can also provide a necessary watchful attitude towards the young person thus strengthening the important protective factors against depression.

A secure attachment of the young person to parents and to peers is vitally important through informal and formal links with parents and other adults. Teachers can build up their relationships with the child and become aware of the vulnerabilities within the child and make assessments of whether or not the young person is aware of their own difficulties, how they spend their time, how well they are able to take care of themselves and how well they use the peer group for support.

A partnership of teachers and parents working together to help the young person is a powerful preventative tool and the partners can work in the knowledge that they have behind them skilled school counsellors, education welfare officers, social workers, educational psychologists and the opportunity for referral to child psychiatric teams and family therapy where necessary.

Mobilisation of the young person's peer group at times of particular stress can be a powerful protective force. If the young person's peers are aware that the child has experienced a recent loss or separation then they can be mobilised to provide important peer group support. They thereby lessen the depressive reaction by modifying the sense of loss that the young person feels when facing the threatened loss of a parent through prolonged illness or through extended marital conflict.

It is amazing how some children manage to escape the quite negative influences of being reared by depressed or alcoholic parents. This protection seems to come from the influence of other healthy adults who have a major role in rearing the child. It can be the healthy other partner, grandparent, neighbour or teacher.

In all situations it is important for parents and teachers to feel that they have the opportunity of an ongoing relationship with health professionals who can be called in preventatively for informal consultations as problems arise. They can help to make the appropriate decision as to when to refer on for further professional advice.

Referral

When should a child be referred to a mental health professional?

a) Parents are notoriously bad at understanding the depressive feelings of their children. Parent-child agreement on depressive feelings is not impressive and parents tend to underestimate how depressed their children are feeling. Parents tend to rarely report the presence of depressive feelings in a child when the child has not reported them direct. When a parent is complaining about depressive feelings in their child, one should always take it seriously.

Children are clearly more likely to give accurate reports of symptoms related to their own internal experiences whilst the parents are better informants of overt behaviour presented by the children. It is therefore important to rely not only on the reporting of the parents but also upon the direct presentation of the child.

b)   Poor school performance and attendance should be picked up early and where this is having a major impact upon the functioning of the child referral on for emotional support and advice becomes essential.

c)   Suicidal thoughts and suicidal attempts should always be taken seriously. Every child who talks about suicide or attempts suicide should be referred. When a child has attempted suicide overnight admission for assessment is often an important cautionary measure to consider.

d)   Children under twelve with clearly depressive symptomatology are not common. They should however always be referred on for assessment and advice.

e)   Where there is a strong family history of major depressive disorder or bipolar affective disorder then the child or adolescent and their family should be referred for assessment.

Therapies – by mental health professionals

Individual therapy for the child will initially support the child through their difficulties and later on work is required to address the underlying mechanisms and causes of the depression: psychotherapy, play therapy, drama therapy and social skills training are all important. The latter particularly is designed to improve peer group attachment which is an important protective factor against the recurrence of depression and can be used in association with relaxation.

Anti-depressant medication can be helpful but is not the main focus of treatment. Anti-depressants should only be given when combined with psychotherapy. Child psychiatrists are very careful when giving medication to children mainly because it tends to treat the symptoms and not the underlying cause. Anti-depressants themselves have a number of side effects which may be harmful to children and adolescents and the tablets may be used by the young person for a suicidal attempt.

Family: it is important to direct help to the parents and the family as well as the individual child. The parents gain insight into their child's problems and feelings. They receive guidance on how to help the child avoid similar patterns of depressive reaction and knowledge of how to deal with their own feelings of impotence in the presence of a child or adolescent who is actually depressed.

Family therapy is often required to break the pattern of scapegoating in the family, which may be a causative or reinforcing factor for the depression in the child.

References

Allen D M. Tannowski K J 1989 Depressive Characteristics of Physically Abused Children. *J. Abn. Child Psychol* 17: 1–11

Angoid A 1988 Childhood and Adolescent Depression I: Epidemiological and Aetiological Aspects. *British Journal of Psychiatry* 152: 601–17

Angold A 1988 Childhood and Adolescent Depression II: Research in Clinical Populations *British Journal of Psychiatry* 153: 476–92

Armsden Gay C. McCauley E. Greenberg M T. Burke D M. Mitchel J R 1990 Parent and Peer Attachment in Early Adolescent Depression. *J. Abn. Child Psychol* 18 (6): 683–97

Barrett M L et al 1991 Diagnosing Childhood Depression. Who should be interviewed – Parent or Child? The Newcastle Child Depression Project. *British Journal of Psychiatry* 159 (11): 7–47

Bowlby J 1960 Childhood Mourning and its Implications for Psychiatry. *Am. J. Psychiatry* 18: 481–98

de Witte H F J 1986 Stemmingstoornissen en Suicide. In Sanders-Woudstra J A R *Leerboek kinder-en jeugdpsychiatrie* pp 467–507

Dolgan J I 1990 Depression in Children. *Paediatric Annals* 19(1): 45–50

Dolto F 1988 *La cause des adolescents* pp 16–17

Elliott D J. Tannowski K J 1990 Depressive Characteristics of Sexually Abused Children. *Child psychiatry and human development* 21(1):

Goodyer I. Wright C. Altham P 1990 The Friendship and Recent Life Events of Anxious and Depressed School Age Children. *British Journal of Psychiatry* 156: 689–98

Kazdin A E 1989. *Childhood depression* pp 121–60

Kelly G L 1991 Childhood Depression and Suicide. *Nurs. Clin. North America* 26(3): 545–58

Keneally P Children's Strategies for Coping with Depression. *Behaviour Res. Ther.* 189; 27(1): 27–34

Rutter M 1985 Psychopathology and Development Links between Childhood and Adult Life. *Child and Adolescent Psychiatry*, 722–94

Seagull E A 1990 Childhood Depression. *Curr. Probl. Paediatric.* 707–55.

4 Whose body? Helping children cope with eating disorders

What is an eating disorder?

Eating, as one of the most basic of human functions, is also one of the most public and most symbolic of bodily activities. Although we eat in order to survive we also use food and eating for purposes of communication, maintaining groupings in society and as part of the various rituals that govern our everyday lives. Most significant life events, be they secular or religious, are marked in some way or other by either the consumption of special food or the prohibition of it. Examples of the former include the wedding feast, the feast on a religious occasion, such as Christmas or the Passover, whilst examples of the latter including giving up certain foods for Lent or fasting from dawn to dusk during Ramadan. Even in a school setting food has its special significance, for example the way in which, in most schools, children still sit down to lunch together, thus encouraging and cementing social groupings and, in many schools, teachers still sit at the head of tables or separately on a high table, thus reiterating the hierarchy on which the school's organisation is based.

Normal eating, therefore, is often a public affair. Disordered eating, however, is more usually a very private one. This means that it is often difficult to identify children with disordered eating, other perhaps than by the fact that, unlike most of their colleagues, their eating is hidden and thus they may absent themselves from or restrict their participation in, the various activities in which eating forms an important part. A further difficulty in identifying the child who has an eating disorder is that of deciding what is actually disordered eating and what falls within the normal wide range of eating patterns that exist across different cultures and even across different families in the same culture. In some families, for example, it is quite normal for food items to be served up one at a time, rather than the more common pattern of meat and several vegetables being served on the same plate. Other families have no clearly identifiable pattern of three square meals a day, but rather eat small amounts and often, following an eating pattern which has sometimes been referred to as 'grazing'. Some people eat quite quickly, others rather slowly and not everybody adheres to the same overall diet, so that, in a school setting, one can expect to find children who are quite omnivorous at one end of the spectrum and others who are vegan and thus surviving on quite restrictive diets at the other. In addition to this there are also those children who have to consume special diets for medical reasons, the most common of these being the diabetic child who has to restrict sugar intake, or the child with Crohn's disease who needs to avoid foods containing gluten.

There are, however, a number of key differences between those children whose eating is unusual but remains within the realms of normality for the population as a whole and those children suffering from a genuine eating disorder. The most obvious of these is the way in which children with an eating disorder have an eating pattern that is significantly different from that of the rest of their family or that expected in their cultural background. Another important difference is the way in which eating disordered children differ significantly from their peers in the quantity of food that they eat, a difference which is usually reflected in their weight and hence physical appearance. Another difference which may be less easy to identify, but which is crucial when deciding whether, or not, a serious eating disorder is present, is that, unlike normal children, most children with a significant eating disorder will not only have unusual eating behaviour, but they will also have unusual beliefs or attitudes about food. On the whole it is these different beliefs and attitudes which help classify eating disordered children into the different types of eating disorder.

Anorexia nervosa

This condition which results in persistent self-starvation leading to extreme emaciation is the commonest serious eating disorder likely to be encountered in a school setting. It has been estimated that in independent schools this disorder affects approximately one in every two hundred girls and when independent schools and state schools are considered together, the prevalence is around one in two hundred and fifty girls. This prevalence increases somewhat in girls over sixteen and hence in schools the condition is at its commonest in sixth forms or sixth form colleges. Approximately one in ten patients referred for treatment with anorexia nervosa are boys.

There have been many attempts to define precisely what anorexia nervosa is and to identify its most important diagnostic features. Ultimately, the condition is a disordered belief about food and eating, together with the physical and psychological consequences of putting that belief into practice. Children suffering from anorexia nervosa have acquired the core belief that their own self-worth is almost entirely dependent on their ability to control their body weight and shape, coupled with the belief that the ideal state is that of extreme thinness. Once the young person starts to behave in a way which is commensurate with this belief system, then weight loss begins and will often continue until the child is extremely physically ill or even dies, unless somebody intervenes (the death rate for anorexia nervosa varies between 5 and 20 percent in different research studies). Anorexia nervosa is, therefore, usually diagnosed when the patient has lost a significant amount of weight (20 percent or more below average weight for height, sex and age), has a strong belief that weight gain would bring about disaster and that extreme thinness is the most desirable goal and these beliefs cannot be shaken by usual approaches to persuasion or coercion. Most doctors would also attach significant importance to amenorrhoea (loss of menstrual periods) and behaviours other than self-starvation which are clearly calculated to promote weight loss, for example, self-induced vomiting, the taking of large quantities of laxatives or indulging in excessive amounts of exercise.

Bulimic disorders

Some children and young people with an eating disorder may consume large quantities of food at a single sitting which some may then vomit back, either spontaneously or having induced vomiting themselves. This consumption of large quantities of food in one go is called bulimia. Although many children and young people may consume a number of cakes or chocolate bars in one sitting as part of their normal eating behaviour, those with bulimia will consume the equivalent of eight or ten, or even more, chocolate bars at one sitting and will do this on a regular basis, often several times a day. Some of these youngsters will actually be suffering from anorexia nervosa so that in between their episodes of bulimia they will be practising self-starvation, often together with other methods of promoting weight loss. For these children it is as if, momentarily, they have thrown caution to the wind and given up their iron control of eating and thus experience a bulimic over-compensation. Others, however, do not make any other attempt to control their weight or shape, and in particular, do not indulge in self-starvation. They do, however, have a belief that control of their weight and shape is of paramount importance but, unlike the anorexic, they are not usually aiming for a state of extreme thinness. The patients who present in this way are said to be suffering from bulimia nervosa as opposed to anorexia nervosa. Those who have bulimia in addition to the features of anorexia nervosa are usually diagnosed as suffering from anorexia nervosa but are said to have bulimia as a complication of it.

Anxiety based eating problems

There is a complex relationship between anxiety and eating. Most of us find that our eating is affected in some way or other if we are extremely anxious or worried, for example about a forthcoming examination, or interview. In this situation some of us will go off our food and others will comfort-eat. This is even more common in children than in adults and explains why most chronically anxious children are either chronically thin or obese. Such children will usually demonstrate other signs of anxiety, for example, frequent complaints of aches and pains, episodes of sweating and shaking, episodes of acute fear associated with running away from a situation, or attempting to run away (panic attacks), erratic attendance at school, and poor academic performance. Usually these children are shy and sensitive and have few friends. Their tendency to over-eat or under-eat is often less marked at home than in school, although this is not always the case. These children will have normal beliefs about eating and food and will often be concerned about their weight gain or loss, unlike, for example, anorexic children who in addition to their unusual beliefs about food, will also have the belief that they should lose more weight.

A second group of children where food and anxiety are related in an important way are those whose anxieties are specifically about food and, therefore, they fail to eat sufficiently because of worries such as the food might be contaminated either by poison substances or by germs. Frequently, these children will have acquired their concerns about food being unsafe either from parents who also have food anxieties or as a result of something they have been taught in school, but have not properly under-stood. Often this kind of food anxiety has a sudden onset and so might be responsible for an abrupt change in a child's eating habits. Unlike children with anorexia nervosa, however, the erroneous beliefs of these children are usually fairly easily dealt with and are not adhered to as rigidly as the anorexic's belief that thin is the only way to be.

Obsessional eating disorders

Although relatively rare, eating problems associated with obsessional illness in children can be quite dramatic and hence fairly
easily spotted. These children will often have a wide range of
obsessional activities, of which their obsessions around food and
eating play only a small part. These children usually believe that
unless they carry out particular, apparently illogical, acts then
something dreadful will happen. Commonly, such children have
obsessions such as the need to touch light switches several times
before leaving rooms, checking that doors are closed several times
before walking away from them, touching particular special places
on walls or stairways several times as they pass and so on. Often
their obsession will be reflected in their academic work and often it
will interfere markedly with their peer group relationships as well.
Their weight loss usually arises from the length of time that it takes
them to eat a meal because of the various obsessional acts that
they need to perform as part of their eating ritual. In a school
setting, where the time put aside for eating lunch is usually fixed
and relatively short, these children fail to eat sufficient food to
maintain an adequate body weight. Although it does occasionally
happen it is unusual for such children to restrict their obsessional
activities to school alone and hence their parents will already be
quite worried about them by the time anybody in school notices
the problem.

Other eating disorders

Perhaps the commonest disorder of eating within schools, in a
Western culture at least, is that of over-eating leading to obesity.
Apart from those cases where such over-eating is associated with a
need to deal with anxiety or adversity, as described previously,
such youngsters cannot really be said to be suffering from an
eating disorder insomuch as their over-eating is, usually, a learnt
behaviour which they have acquired from a family where obesity
and eating larger quantities of food than average is the norm.
Unlike other eating problems, much has been written about the
management of child obesity and, in particular, about the need to
educate parents as much as children, around sensible eating and so
this subject will not be discussed in detail here.

There are, however, other forms of eating problem about which little is written but which do crop up from time to time in schools. These are the eating disorders which arise as a result of a physical disorder which has a direct effect on motivation around eating. The commonest of these is represented by those children who have sustained damage to the part of the brain which controls motivation for eating, either as a result of a head injury or as a result of an operation on the brain to remove a malignant tumour occurring at the base of the brain close to the appetite and eating control centres. The result of such physical insult to the brain can be that the child has no appetite at all and thus gains no pleasure from eating nor knows when to eat. Alternatively, the child's ability to control eating and, in particular, to identify satiety, disappears, hence these children feel hungry all the time and, unless stopped, will eat continuously and will beg, steal or borrow food whenever there is an opportunity. Rarely, a child may have similar difficulties knowing when to stop eating as a result of a genetic disorder, most usually a condition known as Prader Willi Syndrome, which is also associated with varying degrees of learning disorder.

There are a few children who seem to be born without adequate smell and taste sensations. These children usually have feeding difficulties from birth onwards and are of chronically low weight and thus are a significant cause for concern both at home and in school. This condition, which has been called 'Congenital Anosmia' (born with no sense of smell), is not usually associated with any other disability, and as such youngsters require extra help in school at meal times in the context of mainstream education, as opposed to those with Prader Willi Syndrome whose eating problems are usually managed as a part of a wider programme of treatment and education within a special school setting. Fortunately, children with Congenital Anosmia seem to improve considerably as they grow older and thus by the time they enter secondary education, they are usually eating quite normally. Children whose under-eating or over-eating is as a result of brain damage, however, often improve a little during the two years or so following the insult to the brain, but commonly, their eating problem is a life-long one which is very difficult to influence.

Spotting a child with an eating problem at school

Unlike many childhood problems that crop up in school, and which manifest themselves in an obvious and easily identifiable way, for example, temper tantrums or aggressive behaviour, most eating disorders by their very nature are private and thus hidden from view. Within a school setting, they are more likely to be spotted as a result of their consequences rather than because a teacher notices abnormal eating behaviour as such. Sometimes conditions such as anorexia nervosa will come to light as a result of an intimate friend of the sufferer becoming so concerned about what is happening that they inform a member of staff. Usually, however, it is a matter of spotting the warning signs and then investigating further.

Anorexia nervosa

As can be seen from Table 1, anorexia nervosa has physical, psychological, social and academic consequences, any of which might be noticed within school, either in a classroom setting or during other school-based activities, for example sports or drama. Teachers who regularly supervise children undressing, or undertaking activities in close-fitting clothing such as during dance or aerobics, will notice the effects of weight loss, including the stick like appearance, haggard looks, lanugo hair (a fine, downy hair which replaces normal body hair in extreme starvation states), pallor of the skin and cold, blue extremities. Any member of staff might notice a child wearing baggy and apparently ill-fitting clothing and might also notice the sensitivity to cold of the anorexic, resulting in huddling against radiators and wearing multiple layers of clothing, even during fairly warm weather. All of these physical changes result directly from self starvation and also, occasionally, occur when there has been considerable weight loss which has not been self-induced, for example, in children with chronic illnesses. These children, however, will usually have already been identified within school as suffering from a chronic illness and so should not be too easily confused with those suffering from anorexia nervosa.

In order to understand the psychological, social and academic consequences of anorexia nervosa, it is important to be aware of the specific effects of starvation on brain functioning. The human brain is particularly sensitive to starvation and when youngsters have lost 20 percent or more of their body weight they start to exhibit signs of a reversible brain failure. This results in a gradual shutting down of brain functioning in a fairly predictable sequence (see Table 2). A reduction in the ability to use abstract concepts is followed by an increasing inability to think logically and these two problems, whilst unlikely to be noticed by the sufferer, may well

Table 1   Main features of anorexia nervosa

Physical	Psychological	Social	Academic
Obvious weight loss	Very conscious of appearance	Isolated	Works to the exclusion of all else
Wasting of face and hands	Avoids food	Loss of friends	
	Runs self down	Avoids eating situations	Gradual academic failure
Stick-like limbs	May appear depressed	May steal or shop-lift	Falls behind due to periods 'off sick'
Clothes too big			
Periods cease	May self-harm (e.g. overdoses)	May hoard food	
Cold, blue extremities	Irritable	Competitive	
Ashen face with bright eyes	May binge and/or induce vomiting	Withdraws from non-academic activities	
Highly active but may tire easily	Obsessional behaviour		
Exercises excessively	May abuse laxatives		

Table 2 Anorexic brain failure

Loss of ability to use abstract concepts Loss of mathematical abilities Reduction in understanding of logic Problems in relationships Coarsening of personality Failure of relationships Reduction of number of concepts handled Extremes of ideas only handled Single issue only considered Disruption of memory Disorientation in time and space Death	Increasing weight loss ↓

be picked up by teaching staff in subjects such as mathematics, sciences or computer studies. As brain functioning diminishes further the ability to relate to others becomes compromised and this might be noticed as an apparent personality change resulting in a coarsening of personality and a heightening of the most dominant personality features previously present, at the expense of the rest. This results, for example, in a mildly irritable child developing a somewhat explosive personality or a rather shy sensitive child withdrawing totally from relationships.

Further deterioration in brain functioning results in a reduction in the number of concepts which the youngster can handle at any given point resulting, ultimately, in only one or two issues, usually food and self image, being considered at all. This has the effect of reducing the child's conversation to food-related subjects only with the consequence that most of their friends desert them and thus they become isolated within school. A further effect of this deterioration is a loss of the ability to see issues from a range of perspectives leaving only the ability to see issues from the point of view of two extremes. This results in what has been called 'black and white thinking', where each issue is seen as either all good or all bad with a total loss of the ability to see the grey shades in between. Since, by this time, the anorexic has reduced the number of issues they can handle to only one or two, the key one of which is food and its effect on weight, the net result of all this is a child who not only thinks almost exclusively about food, but also sees eating as a wicked thing, starvation as a highly laudable one, weight gain as an absolutely dreadful state and thinness as a highly desirable one.

Although this progressive reduction in brain functioning is a consequence of starvation, irrespective of cause, for the anorexic, it results in a state of mind which compounds the problem and strengthens the youngster's resolve to starve further. This results in a vicious circle or 'whirlpool' of events from which the child is usually unable to escape, without firm help from adults. As Figure 1 shows, the greater the weight loss the greater the degree of brain failure, therefore, the more likely it is that the resolve to starve will be strengthened and hence further starvation, leading to further brain failure and so on. Most of the psychological and academic consequences of anorexia nervosa follow from this and it is easy to see how such changes will lead to progressive academic failure as well as progressive failure in social relationships.

Figure 1   The anorexic whirlpool

Increasing 'brain failure' leads
to stronger resolve to lose weight

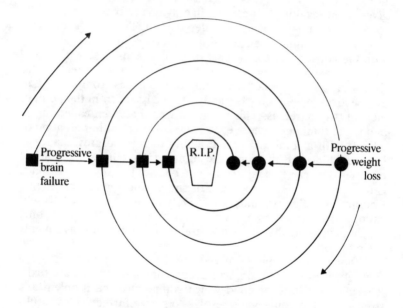

Increasing weight loss
leads to increasing 'brain failure'

Figure adapted from Slade R 1984 *Anorexia nervosa.* Harper &
Row

Bulimic disorders

Since significant weight loss is unusual in bulimic disorders which do not arise out of anorexia nervosa, the various physical and psychological consequences outlined above are usually absent. Youngsters with bulimia nervosa sometimes suffer from poor health and, in particular, poor dental health resulting from the effects of stomach acid on the teeth arising from frequent self-induced vomiting. Teachers might also notice other effects of self-induced vomiting, for example, the presence of dry vomit on clothing and injuries to the fingers resulting from thrusting them into the back of the throat. Staff might also notice significant absences during the school day when the youngster is either binging or vomiting. Occasionally, large quantities of food might come to light, either hidden in a desk or locker and also some bulimic patients secretly vomit in similar places, rather than draw attention to themselves by vomiting in the toilets.

Because of the poor self image which bulimic patients share with those suffering from anorexia nervosa, bulimic children may well exhibit signs of poor self esteem such as being dissatisfied by academic results in spite of being high achievers and being rather isolated and friendless children who find it difficult to cope with peer group relationships.

Anxiety-based eating problems

Children with eating difficulties arising from generalised anxiety can usually be identified from the effects of that anxiety rather than as a result of the eating problem per se. Those whose concerns are restricted to food, however, might only be noticed because of weight loss or because they have stopped eating properly at lunchtime in a rather abrupt way. They may also come to light because their friends have become aware of their worries about food and, in particular, contamination of food. This may also become apparent during the teaching of certain subjects, in particular home economics, environmental studies and biological sciences.

Such children may ask a disproportionate number of questions around issues of food safety and hygiene, whilst not showing the same particular interests in other aspects of the subject.

Obsessional eating disorder

Here again, the eating problem may be less noticeable than the more generalised tendency towards obsessions and ritualistic behaviour. Lunchtime supervisors, however, may well notice the rather unusual behaviour around eating which these children show, for example, touching knives and forks several times before using them, eating food items in a particular and rigid order and touching food with the lips several times before putting it in the mouth. Some obsessional children also need to push the food around the plate in a ritualistic kind of manner, before actually eating it. All of this is likely to result in an excessive length of time being taken to eat a meal so that the time allocated for eating lunch has ended before the child has got even half way through the first course. If this kind of thing is happening regularly and the child is clearly not suffering from anorexia nervosa, then an obsessional eating problem should be suspected, even if the child does not seem to be obsessional in other situations.

Other eating disorders

Children with eating problems resulting from brain damage are likely to have been clearly identified as such well before their return to school following their injury or operation. It is, however, important that staff are aware of the particular difficulties of these children with no sense of satiety who, if allowed, will eat almost continuously. The way in which they take food and money from other children can cause considerable disruption in school and it is likely to be noticed rapidly by everybody.

What the teacher can do

Having identified a child who may be suffering from one of the eating disorders previously mentioned in this chapter, there are a number of courses of action open to teachers which can ultimately lead to the successful resolution of the situation. Once a teacher is suspicious that a child may have an eating disorder, it is important to share that information with other members of staff and with other professionals who work in the school setting. School nurses, educational psychologists, school social workers and education welfare officers may be able to support the members of the teaching staff in deciding on a course of action. If concerns about anorexia or any other eating disorder are increased as a result of these discussions, then it is almost always appropriate for such concerns to be shared with parents or carers. It is also important that a member of the school's staff discusses with the child concerns arising from severe dieting and weight loss.

As in other situations mentioned in this book, it is important for one member of staff in whom the child has trust to be involved in confronting the young person with the situation as it is seen by the adults. It is important that this interview is carried out in a firm but sympathetic manner and in particular that the various excuses for weight loss, abnormal eating behaviour, excessive exercising and disappearances to the toilet are not too readily accepted by the adults expressing concern.

If at all possible, the pupil should be persuaded to accept a medical assessment, either by their own family doctor, or by the school medical officer. This assessment would enable the doctor to decide on the seriousness of the situation. If, following the medical assessment, there are serious concerns about physical health, then it is likely that the doctor concerned will refer the child on to local specialist services for example, paediatrics or child psychiatry.

Meanwhile, it is important for an identified key worker within the school staff to be identified and to speak with the doctor concerned in order to decide what activities may or may not be appropriate for the pupil on the basis of weight gain or loss. This can lead to an agreement with the young person about what the school are or are not prepared to take, for example in subjects such as physical education or drama.

Children with eating disorders, and in particular anorexia or bulimia, will usually be pupils who have not up until now been readily identified as needing special support in school. Usually they will have been high achievers and often will have not given any rise for concern regarding social behaviour in the school. It is, therefore, important that such children receive continuous and systematic support in the school setting and positive feedback for all the things that they do in school, even the most mundane.

It is also helpful for teaching staff to be vigilant about other pupils teasing the child with an eating disorder particularly around weight loss or gain and shape issues. Such teasing is frequently a precipitant for the eating disorder in the first place.

Friends can be most helpful to the bulimic child in monitoring what is going on and in influencing whether they are bingeing or not.

It is also important to boost the young person's self esteem and help them to find ways to feel good about themselves other than through issues around eating.

As far as anxiety based eating disorders are concerned, they too can be helped by a key member of staff, for example a home economics or biology teacher, who can talk them through their anxieties in a logical and rational manner and perhaps direct them towards written material that is likely to alleviate some of their special concerns. The child is, also, likely to be helped by a more thorough understanding of the principles behind cooking and food preparation techniques. Such pupils are often the same pupils who suffer from anxiety in a more generalised way, particularly at examination times and thus often benefit from help around how to manage the anxiety as a condition in itself. Often this can be facilitated by a referral to the educational psychology service who can advise the school and the pupil about techniques which will help in reducing anxiety levels.

Pupils whose eating problems seem to be of the obsessional type should ideally be referred to a child psychiatrist or clinical psychologist since the management of such obsessional behaviour is fairly specialist and the expertise required is unlikely to exist within the school system. Such youngsters often feel that they may be going mad, and so before they are seen by a child psychiatrist or clinical psychologist it is important that they are reassured that such a referral does not indicate that either their parents or the school staff think that they are suffering from a mental illness, but rather that a specialist will be able to teach them particular techniques which will enable them to deal with their compulsions.

The management of children whose eating disorder is organic in origin is again a potentially complex matter. Such children may already be involved with a range of professionals and the school will be made aware of the special help when the child enters school in the first place. School staff have particular difficulties in managing these children, especially those who have hyperphagia (permanent appetite) who beg, borrow and steal food. In such situations it is usually helpful to call a case conference within the school so the matter can be discussed with parents and other professionals involved. This can lead to specific management plans being made based on advice from professionals who have an understanding of the precise nature of the eating problem. Such children often need special support within school, most particularly at mealtimes and may well need to be assessed for a Statement of Special Educational Needs under the 1981 Education Act.

Talking to parents

Parents of most children suffering from an eating disorder are likely to be aware that there is a problem but may not have tackled it directly. This is particularly true in families where a child has anorexia since one of the well known features of such families is the difficulty that family members have in communicating openly with each other. It is very important that parents are involved in discussions about their children and concerns that school staff have about them. Parents will already be worried about eating patterns within the family and discussions around what they have noticed at home are likely to be very useful. If parents have no concerns at all then a more gentle approach may be indicated. One way forward in this situation is to emphasise the way in which the young person concerned is highly valued in school and that certain members of staff have begun to worry about the child's well-being, for instance because they have noticed weight loss or they have noticed the fall off in academic performance.

Some parents may have already tried to seek help for their child with an eating disorder but may well have been met with a firm rejection of such help, for example, a refusal by a child to attend the family doctor. In this situation school staff can support parents, by talking to the child with them and also by making various activities in school contingent on the youngster agreeing to the parents' wishes that medical advice might be sought. It is important to remember that an anorexic child may not have caused parents concern in the past, as many are perceived by their parents as the ideal or perfect children. Although there is a connection between family relationships, family ethos and some eating disorders, it is often appropriate and indeed helpful to put forward clearly that the child with an eating disorder is not necessarily suffering due to faulty upbringing or any specific actions the parents have taken. It is important that teachers involved do not feel that it is the parents' fault or the child's fault either.

Even when professionals are involved there are many things that parents and teachers can do together to help the child with an eating disorder. Communication between staff, parents and pupils is very important. A mutual plan for reducing the stress that the child may be under is also helpful and in the case of an anorexic pupil there should be an emphasis on finding ways of helping them feel good about themselves other than through activities associated with controlling weight and shape. Teachers and families can be particularly helpful in helping the child to find new experiences and to reach new goals. This is because recovery seems to be triggered by developing a new interest in life or by meeting somebody with whom the sufferer starts a new relationship.

It is important that teachers, parents and carers are honest and open with the child who has an eating disorder and that nobody says things to the child which might add to their concerns when everyone else is trying to reduce them.

Becoming involved in the treatment package

Often once the professionals have been involved a comprehensive package of treatment and supervision is constructed. School staff will play an important part in this package and the school nurse may have a particular role in this, being able to monitor weight and nutrition and possibly being an appropriate person to undertake regular liaison with parents. The nurse can, also, help the anorexic child understand the physical consequences of starvation for example, which may lead to the cessation of menstruation and the deterioration in skin, hair and nails. For many children with eating disorders a minimum acceptable weight target is set, particularly for the anorexic or bulimic child and the school nurse can monitor this.

In the classroom context, school staff can be very supportive to external professionals engaged in therapy with a child with eating disorders by ensuring that they avoid making statements which might be contrary to the ideas being encouraged in the child's mind by the therapist and to make statements which actually support the therapeutic work.

Encouraging the young person to feel good about other achievements is important, and it is also important to avoid saying anything to the young person which might encourage them to believe that it is important to diet or to be thin or not to be fat.

Youngsters suffering from overeating associated with an organic condition often need quite complex policing within a school setting in order to ensure that they do not have access to either food provided in school or food belonging to other pupils. It is also important to remember that in most schools it is a simple matter to convert money into food and hence it is not only exposure to food in itself that has to be avoided.

School wide issues – prevention

Like many other emotional and psychological difficulties in children and adolescents, those eating disorders which do not have an organic basis are all, to a certain extent, preventable. The prevalence of anorexia nervosa, in particular, within a school population can be influenced by paying attention to those factors that are known to be involved in its causation, many of which are social or educational. It is also possible to reduce the prevalence of other eating disorders by paying particular attention to what happens in the classroom setting and by identifying vulnerable individuals.

In order to influence the prevalence of eating disorders, and in particular anorexia nervosa within a school setting, it is important to have some understanding of what is known about its causation. The disease has at its core the belief that self-image and self-worth are entirely dependent on an ability to control body weight and shape in the direction of being extremely thin.

The media, and in particular magazines and television advertisements aimed at the adolescent age group, persistently promote the image of young women being thin and in many cases suggest that life can only be meaningful if a young person adheres to the philosophy. One effect of this is that over 50 percent of the average class of fifteen and sixteen year old girls will either be on some form of diet or will actively be contemplating one. The diet product industry makes millions each year in promoting thinness for women and this may be very influential in formulating a young person's idea of how she should look.

Other pressures on young people, however, suggest that they should in fact be high achievers and be able to make their own way in the world. Parents and carers may pressurise children into believing this, and this may be particularly so in families where parents have had to work very hard to move up the social and economic scale from the position held by their own parents. Children who develop anorexia nervosa within such families often have certain personality features which ultimately make living within the family ethos difficult. It seems that when these children meet some kind of crisis or failure, the only way in which they feel able to deal with it is to attempt to succeed in some other area which they think will be appreciated by everybody and thus, in our social climate, select control of body weight and shape and then pursue this with all the obsession and tenacity that they might previously have been applying to their academic studies.

There are a range of failure experiences which have been shown to precipitate anorexia nervosa and they include academic failure, sporting failure, illness, failure in an important relationship and perceived failure within the family, for example father losing his job or a family member becoming seriously ill or alcoholic. As can be seen from Figure 2, the vulnerable child who deals with a failure experience by turning to dieting may then feel successful on achieving an initial weight loss and thus will pursue this relentlessly

Figure 2   A 'model' of causation for anorexia nervosa

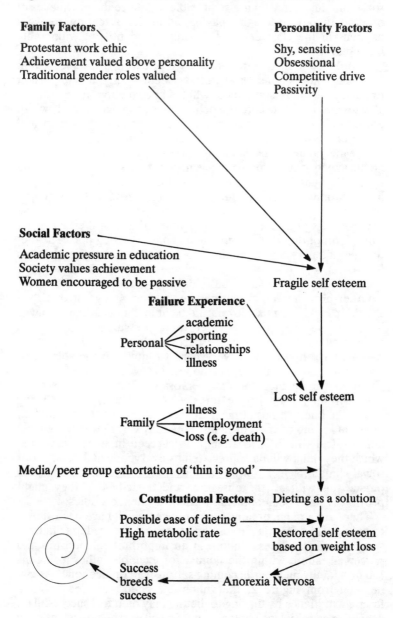

until the psychological effects of starvation take a hold and the condition becomes self-perpetuating and hence increasingly serious.

In order to work towards preventing anorexia nervosa in a school setting there are two main approaches which may be helpful. The first of these is for everyone to be vigilant in identifying high risk individuals and then monitoring them and working with them around many of the issues outlined previously in this chapter. Table 3 lists some of the features which might suggest that a young person is vulnerable in developing an eating disorder.

Table 3   Risk factors for anorexia nervosa

Individual	**Family**
Low self esteem	Upwardly mobile socially
Obsessional personality	Protestant work ethic
Shy/withdrawn	Poor communication about emotions
Passive in relationships	
Highly sensitive to needs of others	Past or present preoccupation with food
Need to compete	Education valued highly in its own right
Need to win or 'be top'	Support traditional 'gender roles'
Preoccupation with media and peer group values	
Sets own standards higher than those set by others	Family members valued more for what they do than who they are
Thrives on success/ devastated by failure	

The other key strategy for prevention is that of paying attention to the ethos of the school and the way in which it might promote the twin messages of thin, pretty and feminine is important for women and academic achievement is everything.

It is particularly important to have a school ethos where youngsters can be valued as much for who they are as for what they can do. It is important to find ways of communicating this ethos to those youngsters who may be at risk from anorexia nervosa, especially when they may not be meeting their own or possibly their parents' academic expectations. It is also important for schools to be offering a breadth of educational experience so that even those youngsters who do not excel in the classroom or on the sportsfield may have access to other activities about which they can feel good.

Eating disordered parents – how the teacher can help

Sometimes, living with somebody who suffers from a severe eating disorder can be as disturbing as being the sufferer oneself. This is particularly true of anorexia or bulimia nervosa, where the sufferer's disordered eating can affect the whole family in a number of ways. Children from such families may well never have experienced a normal eating pattern or a normal family meal. In addition to this, the eating disordered adult will have many of the difficulties outlined in the chapter for eating disordered children, and thus will be disturbed in a number of ways which affect the child. This will include episodes of physical illness as well as episodes of mental disturbance. Children in these families, if they do not understand the nature of their present difficulties, may well feel that they are the cause and frequently their distress about what is happening at home will be reflected in poor academic performance at school, difficult behaviour or even the development of an eating disorder in their own right. A strong family history of anorexia nervosa in particular is a risk for that disorder.

Such children can be much helped by a sympathetic teacher who is aware of their difficulties at home and who is prepared to listen when it may be impossible for the youngster to talk about their confusion regarding their parents to any member of the family. Attention to academic pressures in school can help to ensure that children continue to experience school as a safe haven that is often helpful to them. It is also very helpful to provide them with the kind of information about eating disorders that has already been discussed in this chapter, although it is important to be clear about the nature of the parental eating problem before attempting to educate the child about it.

It is also worth talking to the parent concerned, particularly if the child is showing anxiety or there is any significant difficulty in school. Other professionals can support the teacher in doing this and it may be possible to gain advice and help for that parent from the Eating Disorders Association.

Sources of further help

Further reading

Marilyn Duker and Roger Slade (1988) *Anorexia Nervosa and Bulimia: How to help.* Open University Press

This book offers much advice to anybody trying to help and support a sufferer from either anorexia or bulimia nervosa and also provides further detail about the physical and psychological effects of these conditions and about their causes.

Jill Wellbourne and Joan Purgold (1984) *The eating sickness – Anorexia, Bulimia and the myth of suicide by slimming.* Harvester Press.

This book provides a good understanding of the psychology behind anorexia nervosa and also much practical advice about talking both to anorexics and their families.

Robert Palmer (1989) *Anorexia Nervosa – A guide for sufferers and their families.* Penguin.

This readily available book provides much easily understandable information about anorexia nervosa, albeit from a somewhat medical perspective.

Sara Gilbert (1988) *Pathology of eating – psychology and treatment.* Routledge and Kegan Paul.

Although the title sounds daunting, this book is in fact very readable and provides much information about all eating disorders and their treatment. It is one of the few sources of basic information about the less common eating disorders, described above.

Eating Disorders Association

The Eating Disorders Association is a self-help organisation offering information and understanding through telephone help lines, pamphlets, newsletters and a national network of self-help groups for sufferers from anorexia and bulimia nervosa and their families. They can provide information packs and posters for schools, advertising the help line number or directing children to contact a particular member of staff. The association also provides training for anybody trying to help sufferers from anorexia or bulimia nervosa on a regular basis.

For further details contact: Eating Disorders Association, Sackville Place, 44 Magdalene Street, Norwich NR3 1JE. Tel. 0603 621414.

5 Helping children whose parents suffer with mental health problems

'I'm always going to have that pain in my heart – I try to blank it out but it's always there'. Becky (aged 16).

'I was getting on the bus – someone said "You live in 'C' with that mad woman" – I'm quite calm about it – I used to say "No, she's not my mother" – now I say she is, I say "She has a lot of problems"'. Becky (aged 16).

'Sometimes I think they (his friends) know nothing – because of all the experiences I've been through, I know so much more than them in a way. Lots of kids would be 'phoning Child Line for the things I hear'. Alexander (aged 13).

'Sometimes I cry at night – others can't understand that – they'd rather ignore sleepless nights – crying – it's easier to. I've got a lot of interests, that helps – all the sports I like – cricket – thinking about that and not what's at home. I make sure I get in the school teams. School seems a luxury at times because I've got away from her. I've got such nice friends at school – such nice lads'. Alexander (aged 13).

Personal Communications, 1992.

Introduction

In this chapter I will discuss the possible effects of having a parent with mental health problems and draw out from this some suggestions to teachers. Set in the context of other chapters in this volume, these will be additional guidelines to be added on to the excellent and comprehensive suggestions elsewhere, which relate to bereavement, divorce and other life experiences, and how to assist children through these stressful experiences.

To live with a parent suffering from mental illness does not doom a child to disorder. However, it does not make your childhood, adolescence and finding your place in the world any easier. It has been reported by Gross (1989) that children of mentally ill parents are at greater risk for psychiatric and developmental disorders than are children of well parents, although it is not clear why. Also Gross reports that the parent's diagnosis appears to be less influential in predicting a child's functioning than the severity and chronicity of the illness. Thus it appears that these children are likely to have more than the average need for thoughtful and informed support from other people in their environment, particularly from teachers and others with a long-term and extensive involvement with the child or young person.

Effects on the child

With a mental health problem, particularly in the mother, it is quite likely that a child will be subjected to unstable support, with periods of relatively 'normal' life alternating with periods of crises. Sometimes there may even be traumatic events (for example, violence) or periods which could include the persistent and severe stress entailed in living with a possibly volatile, unpredictable, maybe depressed, maybe manic, maybe explosively angry parent. This may or may not include concomitant marital breakdown, hospitalisation, severe financial problems or other major life crises. These stressors can be of such a severity that it is outside the range of 'normal' experience. However, stressful periods may be interspersed with relatively calm, secure and even happy periods.

You would anticipate that the disruptions and stressors presented by a mentally ill carer who will be, by definition, not functioning adequately as a parent for varying periods of time, would give rise to problems for the child. Problems likely to arise would be fear and anxiety, sleep disturbance, guilt, memory impairment, trouble concentrating, loss of self-esteem and loss of a positive self-image.

Responses to specific and severe 'trauma', and in particular to violence, can best be described as similar to the responses of victims of violence described in post-traumatic stress disorder (PTSD). PTSD involves

(a)   re-experiencing the trauma via intrusive thoughts, dreams or

memories;
(b)   a numbing of responsiveness, demonstrated by constricted emotions, feelings of detachment from others or diminished interest in important activities;
(c)   various physical symptoms such as sleep disturbance and memory impairment.

Fear and anxiety

Anxiety and fear are likely to be strong emotional responses in these children. From an outsider's perspective these two emotional reactions are generally indistinguishable and they show behaviourally in apprehensive expectation, physical tension and vigilance, but it can be useful to distinguish between them for counselling.

In the case of fear, the threat or danger is consciously recognised and generally *external*, and usually the fears are related to physical violation. In contrast, anxiety is more closely associated with psychological violation and does not involve a consciously recognised danger nor an external threat. A better understanding of anxiety can provide important clues to helping children. Unlike fear, the primary threat is *internal* and threats that produce anxiety are related to people's symbolic (cognitive) systems of ideas, values and concepts. When these cognitive systems are disrupted or upset a child is left feeling uncertain and helpless.

Core assumptions (the child's world view)

In general, children and adults appear to develop three funda-mental assumptions about the world;

(a)   the world is benevolent,
(b)   events in the world are meaningful, and
(c)   the self is positive and worthy.

These ideas have been developed by Bowlby, Erikson and others. As a young child's needs are met in their relationship with care givers, this establishes a sense of their security and relative invulnerability in a stable world. A child also develops a sense of self-worth when they are the recipient of positive care-giving. Generally they come to believe that they are not helpless in a hostile environment but capable and cared for in a benevolent world.

It is not difficult to see how very threatening to these basic assumptions of a world that is 'controllable, dependable and just' is the experience of living in close contact with the often topsy-turvy world of a carer who suffers from mental health problems.

Although these psychological aspects of development may appear 'abstract', they are very relevant to the teacher's approach. These children, whose sense of weakness and helplessness is exacerbated in the face of their parents' actions, are apt to experience their helplessness as humiliation, shame and a loss of self-respect. To help them it is important to be aware of the damage to their 'core beliefs' and world view.

Coping and 'puzzling' reactions

Coping with the problems previously discussed is helped by the well-known factors of: social support by other family members, friends, teachers and others. Outside interests, hobbies and an area of interest in which a child can show mastery or 'control' and succeed, such as sport, drama, looking after a pet and so on, can also be extremely helpful and positive. The child will also need a sense of continuity, stability and predictability in the routines of everyday life. Demands on a child should be tailored particularly carefully so as not to exceed their abilities, which may be stretched in the short term just to 'turn up' and keep going.

However, at a more complex level it is useful for teachers to be aware of what 'coping' means with reference to the 'core beliefs' or 'world view' described above. 'Coping' effectively means starting to come to terms with anxiety and with all of its emotional, physiological and behavioural manifestations. This anxiety reflects the disruptions in core beliefs and world view (cognitive systems) – and the road to adjustment and decreased anxiety lies along rebuilding and re-organising these core beliefs or assumptions.

This puts the focus on the child's internal world and their reaction to traumatic events. Looked at from this internal reality some 'puzzling' attitudes of 'denial' can be natural and necessary, although it can be incomprehensible and seem maladaptive from an outsider's perspective. Denial allows a child to slowly and gradually face the realities of an almost 'unbearable' situation and helps their adaptation whilst they are slowly building and rebuilding their world view to incorporate traumas. An example of this is when a child regards a violent parent positively, this being able to maintain a belief in a benevolent environment in which their own safety and security are maximised. Denial means that their situation appears relatively benign, thereby minimising the considerable fears and anxiety associated with their predicament. This helps whilst adjusting to recognition that things are not benevolent, meaningful and just.

Another puzzling phenomenon is guilt and self-blame. But by seeing themselves as in some way guilty, it helps to resolve the question of why injury was meted out to themselves rather than to another. And similarly, self-blame may be adaptive in helping a child to minimise their perceptions of vulnerability – by allowing them to believe that if they alter their behaviours in the future, they will minimise a recurrence of whatever unhappy event they feel they have provoked.

These factors concerning the child's defence mechanisms are important as protection to the child whilst they are trying to maintain cognitive stability and until they can gradually build up an adapted world view. Thus, it is crucial that any counselling or support does not seek to dismantle or change their views prematurely – instead, to listen, listen and then listen further and not to argue with the child's temporary perspectives as his cognitions change and develop.

Conclusions and recommendations

In the preceding and subsequent chapters of this book are excellent guidelines for supporting children through stress. Particularly relevant are the details given in the chapter on bereavement, and rather than repeat these here, teachers are referred to these guidelines.

In addition, and particularly relevant to children coping with mental health problems in a parent, the following guidelines are emphasised:

1. If possible ensure that someone knowledgeable about mental health problems (member of the treatment team – perhaps the community psychiatric nurse) has an opportunity to talk with the child and explain the nature of the parent's illness and that they are not the cause of it. Allow any opportunity to express concerns (such as regarding bizarre behaviour) and, if necessary, several sessions may be held so that a child can make sense of the information.
2. If there is a hospitalisation, efforts to maintain the parent-child link, through telephone calls, or letters, can help to maintain the integrity of this relationship with the parent, in the child's interest.
3. Any opportunity to allow the child to develop areas in which

they are successful, in control and involved in activities that increase self-esteem, should be assiduously sought – or even 'manufactured'.

4. Recognition and encouragement of the crucial need for support from siblings, friends, the other parent, relatives and 'significant other' adults, teaching staff, neighbours.

5. Recognition that it is emotionally and cognitively beneficial for the child to disclose and be given 'counselling' support in listening to his problems. (Note No. 6 below.) But counselling and listening must be extremely non-directive and aimed at allowing expression and coming to terms with issues not previously explicated.

6. Recognition of the strong need in many children at some times for avoidance and denial of the problems, and respect for this defence. However, the child should be made aware that there will always be a listening ear available should they show any signs of needing this. However, blocking and denial are one means of 'coping' at certain stages and should be recognised as such.

7. Teachers to be aware of the long-term and variable nature of the background problem, so as to be alert to help when suddenly difficulties erupt after seemingly 'trouble-free' times.

References

Buckwalter K. Kerfoot K. Stolley J 1988 Children of Affectively Ill Parents. *Journal of Psychosocial Nursing and Mental Health Services* **26**: 8–14

Gross D 1989 At Risk: Children of the mentally ill. *Journal of Psychosocial Nursing and Mental Health Services* **27**(8): 14–19

Fisher S. Reason J 1988 *Handbook of life stress, cognition and health*. Wiley & Sons

Rutter M 1985 Resilience in the Face of Adversity: Protective Factors and Resilience to Psychiatric Disorder. *British Journal of Psychiatry* **147**: 598–611

6 Children with life threatening illnesses

In this chapter, I would like to look at the various stages in life threatening illnesses and how these not only affect the child, but also the family and concerned adults. I would like to look at the various stages in the illness, that is the period before diagnosis, the time surrounding diagnosis, the period while treatment is under way, the period of recovery and in those situations where there is no recovery, the way in which we can all handle the death of a child and help others to cope.

Pre-diagnosis

Medical science is such that the group of children with life threatening illnesses is minute. Consequently, experience of dealing with them is limited. Many teachers will go through their whole career without having had the experience of a child who has developed a life threatening illness, let alone having the experience of having one of their pupils dying. Many of these conditions are so rare that there often appears to be delay by the medical profession in diagnosing them. A GP can go through his whole career without having a child presented who is likely to die from an illness. Parents and close members of the family sometimes miss early symptoms, as do other adults, but normally the parents do have some appreciation that there has been a marked change in behaviour, or there are clear physical symptoms which need to be reported to the GP. Sometimes the parents have had struggles with professionals to convince them that their child should have further medical tests. They can appear to professionals as being over-anxious. As we all know, the majority of children can go through phases of appearing to be lethargic, inattentive, bad tempered, withdrawn or overactive. The vast majority of this behaviour is coped with by helping the child to adjust to other children and to social situations but also it causes adults to be angry with the child and perhaps punish them, and be critical of them. Sometimes the behaviour does not respond to the normal exercise of behavioural techniques and medical advice is sought. Of the vast majority of cases where medical advice is sought, there is found to be no physical reason for the behaviour and the child needs consistency of care and consistency of rules by which to live. Among those children exhibiting behavioural problems, there will always be a very small group where it is found that there are physical reasons for their behaviour, and occasionally a child will be found to have a life threatening illness.

Time of diagnosis

Good medical practice would indicate that the parents should be aware of the full range of tests that are being undertaken on their child. In fact, there are occasions when doctors are not clear with parents that they are testing for some life threatening illnesses, because they know that the chances of an individual child having such an illness are so slight that they do not want to upset the parents unnecessarily. Consequently when a diagnosis is given to the parents, this can come as a very great shock. Even when the parents have been prepared for a distressing diagnosis, they are naturally in a state of shock when they hear it. Different people react differently in that some will talk volubly about it, while others will not want to speak about it at all. Normally, as soon as the diagnosis is given, the parents and the whole family are jettisoned into a frenzy of activity to make arrangements for intensive treatment for the child and consequently do not have the time or the emotional energy to deal with their initial sense of shock. In addition to the practicalities directly involving the child, their jobs, being with the child in hospital, they also have to work out the involvement of the rest of their children and how the rest of their children will be cared for. In the majority of situations, extended family and close friends are made aware of the situation rapidly. GPs are often informed by a telephone call from the hospital doctor carrying out the tests. The first the teachers will know is by being told on a school morning that the child is absent and the reason for their absence. This information will frequently be imparted just before a teacher has to go to face a class of children and consequently there will be little time for the teacher to deal with their own feelings of shock and bewilderment beforehand.

The teacher, as with other adults, will immediately be feeling sad, shocked, and unable to grasp the situation. Again, as with other adults, there may well be feelings of guilt because they may not have noticed significant differences in the child earlier, and they will often feel guilty that they might have reprimanded the child when the child exhibited unacceptable or unusual behaviour. In an ideal world, the teacher should have the opportunity to discuss this with professional colleagues. Unfortunately, as school life is hectic, there is little time to do this and also as there is such little experience of children with life threatening illnesses, there can be a lack of understanding by colleagues. Bland comments can be made to the teacher having the closest contact with the child, saying that the child is bound to get better or that the teacher does not have anything to worry about in the way they treated the child, and so on. The reality is that the teacher doesn't have anything to reprimand themselves for if they have told a child off, and subsequently found that the child is ill. We can all only behave to others on the basis of the actual knowledge we have of another person, and, as the teacher could not have possibly known that the child was ill, they would have been wrong in fact to have acted in any other way. The teacher has to be helped to understand that the guilt they are feeling is a very natural reaction to shock and anticipatory grief. At this stage, the teacher does need to have maximum accurate information about the illness from which the child is suffering, the prognosis for that child and the sort of treatment the child is going to have to undergo. When they have this information, they can then be in a position to discuss the way in which they should inform the classmates of the children, with the parents' consent, about the diagnosis.

There are a variety of people who can help with this. Accurate information can be obtained directly from the parents. With the parents' permission, the school can approach the social worker for the hospital in which the child is receiving treatment. If the teacher has not had the opportunity to get the consent of the parents, the social worker will always do this before discussing the medical condition of the child. The social worker will always be willing to come to the school to discuss the situation with the teacher and any other teaching colleagues involved with the child, and to be involved in sharing information with the other children in an appropriate way. In some hospitals, paediatric community liaison nurses are in post. They will be well able to be involved with the school.

Dealing with the ill child throughout treatment

There will obviously be a variety of ways in which children are treated according to their illness. The common thread will be that there will be an initial period in hospital while diagnosis and appropriate treatment is determined. This period in hospital can vary from perhaps a week or two, to many months or periods in hospital, periods back in school, periods back in hospital for sometimes very intensive treatment. Regardless of the length of time that the child is in hospital, the school and school friends are of vital importance, not only in maintaining educative progress, but also in continuing to help them feel part of their social group and also to maintain their own identity. The practice that many teachers have of getting the rest of the class to make and send individual cards to the children is very important to any ill child, but of great importance to a very sick child. The repetition of these cards becomes increasingly important as the child feels that they are losing their grip on their friends, and naturally is losing their place in school and among the friends. Taking into consideration the feelings of the other children, it is exceptionally helpful to the ill child to have visits from their friends. If possible, these visits should be well prepared as children who have been good friends sometimes become very inhibited in the strange setting of the hospital. The ill child needs to have information about what has happened in school, the games that are being played at the time, what happened in the playground and interesting things that the rest of the class has done. Although the child can feel distressed at having missed out on treats, at least they will know when they rejoin the class what has been happening in school and to other children. This contact can be very positive for the ill child who still feels involved and cared for.

Careful work has to be done in collaboration with the parents to discover the explanations parents have given to the child of the illness, so that a consistent picture can be given. A visit from a favourite teacher can help a child to discuss their anxieties. The child may not feel able to discuss these worries with parents who are too close, or a social worker, nursing or medical staff they have just met. In order to be prepared for this eventuality, there is a need for the teacher to keep in mind the truth of the situation, the reality which the child understands and also to have prepared themselves to be honest with the child within the context of the parents' and medical explanation that the child already has been given. There is always the very strong possibility that a child who actually is terminally ill has not been specifically told, and yet they themselves have knowledge that their illness is terminal. No person wants to be the bearer of this sort of information to a child, perhaps more so a teacher who has feelings of affection and care for the child. If a child does ask a direct question as to whether they are dying and has not been told, the reality normally is that the only people who would know this would be the doctors and the nurses, so the teacher can suggest that the child might like to ask the question of their favourite doctor. It is, however, perfectly acceptable for an adult to acknowledge with the child that they are very seriously ill. The emphasis would be on the fact that they are receiving very good medical help which will help them to get better, if it is possible for them to get better. Developing of course from this could well be a discussion about what happens to people when they die and again there is a need for a teacher to try to give a consistent notion of what happens in line with the family beliefs. It can be very valid to say that we do not know exactly and perhaps put the question back to the child to see what their beliefs are.

The reality of telling the child that their illness is life threatening causes not only anguish to adults but also a lot of disagreement. Partly, the disagreement comes from the fact that the possibility of the death of a child is the most difficult concept for an adult to accept. Everything in our nature is geared to protect and nurture children. When a child develops a life threatening disease, whether or not we are parents, we feel that we have failed the child and have failed in our primary task of nurturing. There may be feelings of anger and often this is projected on to others such as the doctors, parents, teachers and even on to the actual child. The acceptable expression of anger on to adults can become very concentrated in the discussion as to whether a child is told of the seriousness of their illness. In telling the child of the reality of the situation an admission is being made that the adult world has failed in its primary task of caring for and protecting the child.

In a situation where a child is attending school, there is naturally the need to understand the physical limitations and help can be obtained in getting accurate information about these through the Senior Community Medical Officer as well as from the parents. Linked in with this is the need to understand the total effect of the treatment on the child. There needs to be an understanding of when the child's behaviour is actually altered by the medication and when it is altered because of uncertainty of re-entry into the class situation, fear of becoming ill again and also when the child is using the illness to avoid doing things that they normally would not have wanted to do.

The classic example is the child who develops severe headaches when presented with a subject that they do not like. The child is in a very powerful position in presenting symptoms associated with the illness. The teacher may feel guilt that they did not identify symptoms at an earlier stage in the pre-diagnostic period, but will need to weigh that against the fact that the child may be using previous symptoms. The symptoms have to be reported and checked out, but strategies have to be worked at to enable the child to gain confidence in dealing with a school situation and gaining the maximum from it.

Naturally, an ill child is not dealt with in isolation. The teacher has the task of explaining the situation to other children in such a way that the other children will deal appropriately with the ill child. The ill child needs to maintain their identity and personality and has to be reintegrated into the class group as rapidly as possible. On the other hand, there might be situations where they have to be dealt with and protected in a way in which they had not before the diagnosis of the illness. Children who have had brain surgery, for example, can initially present as having different personalities from that which they had before. At this stage they can be well able to cope with school, but other children can be bewildered by an apparent change in personality which is normally only temporary. Other children have to experience the fact that the ill child enters and leaves their group and they have to be helped with this. Explanations have to be given to the other children that link in precisely with the explanation given to the child so that in discussing the illness, there is consistency.

Recovery

Any illness of any degree of seriousness has some effect on the child. Life threatening illnesses have a profound effect. In dealing with adolescents, they have had to face the reality of their own death and the anxiety engendered by the treatment. They have frequently had to go through a great deal of pain and know that they might have to cope with further pain associated with further treatment. These issues jettison the adolescent from childhood to adulthood in an unnaturally speedy fashion. Young people who have dealt with these issues sometimes find some difficulty in relating to their peer group as they start feeling that the previous interests can be flippant and irresponsible. They have learnt more than most of us learn in our whole life about themselves, about their family relationships and have developed coping strategies that most of us as adults have not had to bring into play.

At the time of adolescence, when they were looking towards separating from their parents, they have had the additional conflicting situations of maturing rapidly in some areas of their life and yet having to become increasingly dependent for their physical care. In children and young people suffering from cancer or leukaemia, they have had long periods of spending time exclusively with either one or other of their parents and have often had to share a room with their mother for weeks at a time. Most young people will acknowledge readily the conflict that this has engendered, in that they recognise their parents' anxiety and wish to be near them through times of crisis, and the young person themselves want support, but on the other hand they still want to have privacy. This difference in experience is bound to cause tensions between a young person and their peer group. Normally, as time goes on, the rest of the group actually catches up in development with the young ill person. Adults, including teachers, can feel threatened by having to face the reality of death and the maturity of the young person who has been through this experience.

It is often difficult to determine precisely when a child has fully recovered from some conditions. If a child has had meningitis or, even less common, polio, or has had a serious road traffic accident, then naturally the physical recovery time may be more clearly identified. With cancer and leukaemia, treatment takes two years to complete and following that, there continue to be check-ups to ensure that the disease has not become active again. Children who have had a severe physical illness can naturally become wary about contact with other people in case they pick up some other infection, or they can become nervous and frightened if they have had some severe accident. Consequently, teachers are in the situation where a different child has re-entered their class from the one that left it. Other children will be asking questions, which can cause severe distress to the child if the illness has been sudden and quickly recovered from and consequently there has not been time to help the child to deal with some of the psychological implications of having had such an illness. Factual information about the likelihood of the child having a further period of illness can be shared, but the child has lost the basic confidence in security in life which most of us do not face until much later.

As with the ill child who is attending school, the recovered child can continue to present with symptoms which can be very worrying to adults. It is therefore important for the teacher to work closely with naturally anxious parents and with medical staff to identify worrying symptoms or what might be the child under stress or what might be them actually 'playing up'.

Death

In the event of the death of a child following an illness, most adults are shattered. It is possible that the child has continued to attend school to within a few days of their death. Staff and other children can help them to get around the school and it is possible for them to continue enjoying life virtually until becoming unconscious. Other children can see them very ill, as can the teaching staff, and perhaps this helps in coping with their own grief in that death was the natural outcome of this child's illness and discomfort. Other children in the family can also be kept within normality as long as possible, but again can be helped to understand the reality of the situation and can be supported by the other children because they have an understanding of how ill the child was before they died. Perhaps the ill child gave assurances to the other children that one does not die unless there is a good physical reason. In the more usual situations, staff who have been closely linked to the child such as the class teacher or the headteacher, may well have been frequently visiting a child until their death. It will have been useful to other staff and pupils if they can have reported back without causing too much distress about the physical deterioration of the ill child. At this stage, as in other stages, it is important for the messenger from the child to understand the process of the illness so it can be explained to other children. At the time of death, the other children will be asking lots of questions and this should be encouraged. Other children should not be discouraged to talk to brothers and sisters about the dead child. In fact, it is important that the dead child is talked about as somebody that everybody misses and somebody who has joined in the happy times in the class. The penalty for not allowing an atmosphere where the dead child can be talked about regularly is that other children in the class start wondering about their own value if they disappeared from the school. If staff are finding difficulty in coping with this, then advice is always available from either the hospital social worker or the paediatric liaison nurse based at the hospital, or the educational psychology service.

The rules for dealing with children with life threatening illnesses are really basically only those rules that apply in all circumstances. The primary need is for adults dealing with these children to have had the opportunity to think through their own feelings and beliefs and to identify how they can cope with this very demanding situation with honesty, compassion and integrity, to enable the ill child, the other children in their class, and their brothers or sisters, to continue to reach their full potential both during and following the illness.

References

Alex M & B 1983 *Grandpa and me*. Lion
Fabian A 1988 *The Daniel diary*. Grafton
Heegaard M 1988 *Facilitated guide for when someone very special dies*. Woodland Press
Heegaard M 1988 *When someone very special dies*. Woodland Press
Hunter M 1975 *A sound of chariots*. Fontana Lions
Little J 1985 *Mama's going to buy you a mockingbird*. Penguin
Oakhill A 1988 *Supportive care for the child with cancer*. Wright
Smith D B 1986 *A taste of blackberries*. Penguin
Stickney D 1984 *Waterbugs and dragonflies*. Mowbray
Wass H. Corr G 1984 *Helping children cope with death – guidelines and resources*. Hemisphere

7   Supporting the bereaved child at school – feeling at a loss?

Introduction

It is estimated that in Great Britain as many as fifty children a day will lose a parent through bereavement and many more will lose other family members, friends or pets. Other significant losses, for example, through separation or desertion, are now commonplace in our society and the question arises as to what help and practical guidance can be given to teachers who may find themselves in the front line of having to support children in these circumstances. What is the right thing to say when a child is bereaved? What should one do and what different ways are there of providing support? It is a curious fact that in this country few teachers receive formal training in how to help children cope with bereavement or loss and, not surprisingly, it is often claimed that death has now become *the* most important taboo area of the twentieth century; however many 'deaths' children may see on the television it is no longer *experienced* as the commonplace event that it was in, say, Victorian times. Reduced childhood mortality levels, improved medical care, better social conditions and fewer wars now lead us to expect that more and more people in society will enjoy a normal life span. When death does strike, the removal and after-care of the body is now managed with great clinical efficiency which means that fewer people than in former times are likely to see for themselves, to touch or to have direct experience of a dead person. At a more philosophical level, many would claim that within today's society, spiritual values have declined in the face of mounting materialism and that, with the quickening pace of life and our increased concern for living and lifestyles, we may be losing a vital and harmonising sense of our own mortality. There is a paradox in the fact that the world is so often portrayed as full of violence and that children see death on the television and reported in the media, yet in actual fact they will have less real, close experience of death than their forebears. When science and technology have enabled us to gain so much control over our lives, perhaps the reason why death has become such a taboo lies in its stubborn inevitability over which we ultimately have no control.

In the United States, classes in death studies have been pioneered as a proper part of the school social curriculum but in this country, for the most part, the subject has received scant attention. Whether for reasons of its taboo nature or simply because in today's busy classroom teachers have so much else to occupy them, it is unlikely that the psychology of loss and bereavement will occupy a position of much priority in many of our schools. Many people feel that children are more adaptable than adults and quickly get over such losses but according to Bowlby the notion that children's grief is short-lived is quite untrue. Although counselling as a skill can of course be refined and practised, it would be sad and wrong if staff in schools held back from reaching out to children in need because they had not been 'trained'. There is a widespread view that the subject of death and bereavement should not be over-developed as an academic subject nor become the domain of experts but should always be viewed as a basically normal, natural process for which our instinctive reactions as helpers are likely to serve us well. It is hoped that the following notes for guidance will reinforce this common sense view and help teachers to feel more confident to help in such an important area.

Stages of bereavement

It is usual when talking of bereavement to refer to key 'stages' which people often go through following a serious loss, but children, like adults, are individuals and do not always pass through such stages smoothly or in neat linear succession. The final 'stage' of rebuilding for example is never completed as a 'stage' and the implication that bereavement is a matter which one eventually 'gets over' can in fact be both offensive as well as inaccurate; many bereaved people rightly feel that they will never get over their loss and that it would be wrong to do so. It is also commonplace for the earlier stages of bereavement, those marked with particularly strong emotional reactions, to be re-activated later in life, for example by further losses, anniversaries, periods of stress and so on. Parents and teachers should not become anxious because a child has apparently not progressed neatly through the recognised stages of bereavement, since such concern may itself be transmitted to the child who may then think "sometimes I'm feeling depressed, sometimes angry, sometimes sad, but other people seem to be expecting me to be feeling differently so how *should* I be feeling?" Children need reassurance that it is all right to experience the confusion of feeling which often follows a close bereavement and to know that this is part of normal grief. Some children, like some adults, may do much of their grieving privately and this may be the case when a child appears not to be expressing any of the feelings associated with a particular 'stage'.

The four main stages of bereavement often referred to are:–

Shock. This is characterised by a total emotional denial, often misunderstood by others who may comment on how 'well' the bereaved person is coping. In reality the person is operating on a kind of automatic pilot and may go through the normal daily routine but in a kind of dream. This initial shock period may last for a few hours or a few weeks. Mary's father died early one morning and the rest of the family were surprised that Mary not only wanted to go to school as usual but also insisted on going to the school disco that same evening!

Anger and unfairness. This stage is characterised by the feeling 'why me?' or 'why us'. The bereaved person feels angry and may need to accuse or blame someone. At school, a child may have periodic tantrums or be unduly irritable with friends or the teacher. This is an emotional need and not likely to be amenable to logic. Also, at this stage physical symptoms may occur such as problems with digestion, sleep and concentration. There may be ghostly experiences or feelings that the person is not really dead, which may be a way of 'denying' what has occurred.

Sadness, sorrow and longing. During this extended stage, the predominant feelings are those of depression and aloneness; there may be a compulsive need to relive the past and go over recent events as a way of emotionally digesting what has taken place. The bereaved person may wish to be on their own a lot, to cry, go over letters, to look at photographs, to remember; this is an important part of grieving which may be very private.

Rebuilding. Gradually life begins to have some point or purpose again and usually by the end of the first year there is some indication of an attitude of new hope.

The school as a support system

For the bereaved child who may be feeling that their world has suddenly fallen apart, it is important to provide a sense of holding and of security. The importance of having a predictable routine and the part which school can provide in this will be clear. School life with its break times, assemblies, familiar faces, and everyday rituals, can impart a crucial sense of life 'going on', of the world not falling apart. In some families, a bereavement may set in train a number of changes – a house move, change of school, change of jobs, new friends – so that the major loss becomes effectively compounded by a number of additional losses. In some instances such changes may be necessary or unavoidable but from a child's point of view, too many changes may intensify feelings of helplessness or feelings that matters are beyond their control.

Teachers should therefore be aware that the predictability of school life, its routine, rituals and familiarity can all be of intrinsic value and support to the child who has suffered bereavement, particularly when life at home may naturally be in a state of temporary turmoil. In terms of personal relationships, the child who at home may be having to adjust fundamentally to now being an only child, or being a member of a single parent family, may be reassured by still feeling the same member of his peer group at school. In judging such matters, it will clearly help the teacher to talk to a parent or close family relative concerning the bereavement and its impact on the child so that there is good understanding about what has happened, the implications for the future and the co-operation which is needed in terms of giving consistent support.

The role of the teacher

The class teacher who is faced with a bereaved child will first need to have realistic expectations of what should and can be done to help. The feelings of helplessness as bystanders which we all tend to feel at such times, are normal; we would like to be able to remove the pain, to make the situation better for the child and we are inclined to say 'don't cry . . . don't upset yourself' but the pain and upset need to be seen as part of the normal grief reaction. It is a key principle of bereavement work that our role as supporter is to help the bereaved person *through* their pain rather than seeking to remove or avoid it. It is often claimed that in counselling work what you *are* is as important as what you *do* and the teacher's role is to be there, to support, listen, care, sustain and to be a source of strength and stability.

In many instances following a family death the bereaved child is initially likely to be absent from school for a short while. This may enable the class teacher or form tutor to talk to the group about what has happened and what can be done to help. Each member of the group will react individually according to their own experiences of death and bereavement and the sensitive teacher should be aware that certain other children within the group, who may also have encountered loss, may still have deep feelings which have been suppressed and that they too may be in need of some reassurance. Others in the class may be fearing the loss of a loved one and may, at some point, want to talk about their own situation. What is quite likely is that, as a group, the children will be looking to their teacher for a lead as to how to *be* as well as what to do, what to say and how to offer support. Perhaps a group card can be made and signed by the class. This can be a simple ritual which all children understand and can help them feel less helpless as they engage in something positive together. Others may want to write more personally and privately. Warn the class not to swamp the child with too much sympathy when they return to school. Quiet sympathy, a few words of comfort and then basic normality are what most children wish for. Bereaved children often fear that other children are avoiding them and no longer wish to be friends. Tell them this. Encourage the class not to avoid simply because they are embarrassed or because they do not know what to say, and emphasise how hurtful this can feel. Most bereaved children want to be treated as normally as possible and to be included in what is going on. Reassure the class that it is all right and usual for them and adults not to be sure of what to say. Explain that some children want to talk about the bereavement while others do not.

If, as time goes by, a child chooses to talk to you about their bereavement, then this, of course, is a privilege. Try not to be over-concerned about saying the wrong thing. Be attentive, listen carefully and be reassuring. Grief is a normal and universal process, not a subject exclusive to experts nor a subject to be over-theorised or over-medicalised. Remember that most helping and counselling is done by ordinary people.

Finally of course, the teacher needs to be mindful of the child at school who is prone to making cruel remarks. It is a curious fact that not all children are kind and supportive to the child who is bereaved but may actually be openly cruel and capable of hurtful and insensitive remarks. Such children may have been hurt themselves or harbour deep insecurities themselves. The role of the teacher in such cases is to be vigilant, to identify such children and to intervene where necessary.

Language

In counselling work generally, and certainly as far as bereavement work is concerned, there is a need for us all to have a great respect for language – the capability of the right words to be helpful, or the wrong words to be hurtful. It is often said, for example, that platitudinous or philosophical remarks do not help at all. Comments such as 'cheer up', 'don't cry', 'you'll get over it', 'I know how you feel' or 'mummy's depending on you now she hasn't got daddy any more' are more likely to be concerned with *our own* feelings than with those of the child. Unconsciously, we may wish to deny that a child is feeling the pain of bereavement. Bereaved people, young and old, are often offended by the idea that they are expected to 'get over it' or that somebody else really knows how they feel.

Children can be very literal in their use and understanding of language. As adults, we often use images and words euphemistic-ally when talking of death but for younger children, who may interpret our words very literally, there may be a risk of unhelpful fantasies developing as a result. Children are prone to using their imagination to fill in gaps in their understanding. Peter, for example, was upset that his grandfather's 'body' was to be buried and wanted to know what would be happening to the rest of him – his head, arms and legs! Katy developed an anxiety about bedtimes after her pet dog had to be put to 'sleep'. George asked if it was still all right to stroke his cat after his grandmother died 'of a stroke'. We need to ask what sorts of images are conveyed to young children by the language we use – what sort of 'attack' is a heart attack? – how exactly do 'soles' (of shoes?) go to Heaven, and why? What exactly happened when Aunt Mabel was 'taken' and Uncle Tom 'passed over'; and how on earth did great grandfather get 'lost' in the war?!

Nowhere are the limitations of language more apparent than when talking to children about heaven and god. Children with their natural lack of inhibition will often want to know exactly what it is like in heaven, why Jesus wanted daddy to be with him and why they can't go too? What clothes do people wear in heaven and does it rain there? Such conversations can lead to great metaphysical confusions so that we may become hopelessly caught in webs of our own weaving! Rather than risk this it is important for children to know when they have reached the point when the answers to their questions are not known. Quite young children will respect the intellectual honesty which requires us to say sometimes "I don't know the answer to your question . . . some people believe 'x', some people believe 'y' . . . no one knows for sure . . . you must decide what you will believe . . .". At this point it is more helpful to encourage children to develop their own ideas and beliefs rather than giving precise answers which may not be either accurate or honest.

Sorting out feelings

Following a significant bereavement, children and adults are likely to experience a confusion of feelings, which will range from sadness and depression to guilt and anger. It is impossible to predict exactly how an individual child is likely to react. The grieving process is an individual matter and much grieving will be done internally or privately. In general, the class teacher should not expect a pre-determined set of reactions. The individual child may show a greater degree of quietness or else may be more prone to tantrums. Tearfulness may be triggered by seemingly trivial events or there may be greater irritability. There is sometimes a need to '*take it out on*' someone or something. Whereas some children may perform less well at school following a bereavement, others may immerse themselves in their work as a form of distraction or to escape the reality of their loss. There is a clear need on the part of the teacher to show patience, kindness and understanding. Very young children may not have the verbal fluency needed to be able to articulate their feelings and it is for someone – usually a parent – to gently help the child to put into words and give a simple explanation of what has happened and what he may be feeling. Helping a child to identify and label feelings correctly can also help to give increased feelings of control. When language is absent or inadequate for giving expression to feelings, many children will show their feelings more primitively in a variety of ways, through play, drawings, in dreams or in their outward behaviour. Older children may be able to talk to close friends, to keep a diary or write poetry and a caring class teacher may be able to provide opportunities within the curriculum for children to express some of their feelings in these ways.

Early education and the formation of attitudes

A child's ability to sustain and cope with a significant bereavement will be partly determined by experiences which have occurred and attitudes which have been moulded earlier in life. Teachers of young children can significantly help in this preparatory process, particularly if they themselves possess a mature attitude towards the subject of death and are able to talk about such matters simply, honestly and with confidence. Children need to learn that death is a valid subject which can be talked about. There is little doubt that some children, because their questions are not answered, or answered abruptly, or accompanied by a certain ambiguous feeling, learn that death is indeed a taboo subject and best not talked about. But those parents and teachers who are able to answer questions simply and honestly will help to dispel fear and encourage a healthy attitude not only by giving information but by conveying their own positive attitude about the subject. Children also need to learn what being 'dead' *means* and this requires direct experience as well as discussion. Children who have a small pet which has died or discover a dead bird in the garden should be shown that (having due regard for hygiene) it is all right to touch, hold and care for such a creature. Children who are told 'don't touch' or 'don't go near' or who find that their favourite pet has been disposed of unceremoniously and with some secrecy, will be learning something quite different to the child whose family arrange a simple burial ceremony and who express feelings of loss together.

Educating children about death and bereavement

In the normal course of school life opportunities will present themselves for teachers to acknowledge and explain to children death as a normal, natural event. In this way possible 'taboo' feelings associated with death may be replaced with knowledge, reasoned beliefs and an open, healthy attitude, helping children to cope better with personal bereavements when these occur later in their lives. Ways in which this process can be encouraged include the following:

> allowing death or bereavement, as natural events, to be talked about and discussed openly;
> being a good model, as a teacher, in terms of attitudes towards death and serious loss;
> explaining how death in the plant, animal and human kingdom can have positive features linked with evolutionary processes, regeneration and the development of religious beliefs concerning the after-life;
> answering children's questions simply and honestly;

giving basic information and dispelling common fantasies;
describing and explaining the range of feelings which accompany loss and bereavement and how people may react differently;
showing how people can help and support one another in times of sorrow;
explaining how rituals, ceremonies, photographs and mementoes can be important ways of sharing and remembering;
encouraging children to develop a personal belief system;
enabling children to share, sensitively, their experiences, thoughts and feelings about death or loss.

In the normal course of school life there will be many incidents and occasions when the sensitive class teacher will be able to give information and acknowledge the various feelings which are engendered by loss, separation or bereavement. There will be opportunities to show how we need to consider other people's feelings, to be kind and helpful when others are sad. Those who have listened to young children talking about death will be familiar with the wisdom often contained in such comments as that made by eight year old Julie "*just because he's* (her brother) *dead doesn't mean we've got to stop loving him*", or that by six year old Steven who said "*I still talk to Rusty* (the dog) *and it's like he's still alive*".

References

Bowlby J 1979 *The making and breaking of affectional bonds*. Tavistock Publications
Kfir N 1989 *Crisis intervention verbatim*. Hemisphere Pub. Corp.
Kobler-Ross E 1970 *On death and dying*. Tavistock Publications
Krementz J 1986 *How it feels when a parent dies*. Victor Gollancz
Wells R 1988 *Helping children cope with grief*. Sheldon Press

8 Suicide: the unspeakable loss

"I loved my dad. Why wouldn't anyone at home tell me how he really died? Why did my friends at school know before me?"
Michael, aged 12

Introduction

People bereaved as a result of suicide are at a high risk of pathological grief. The death is socially unacceptable which means that there may be little or no support for the grievers. A veil of secrecy may surround the actual cause of death and factors that have contributed to it. In fact perhaps suicide is the most unspeakable loss, leaving grievers with a legacy of shame, fear, rejection, anger and guilt. Suicide calls into question the priority which we give to life and outrages our basic assumptions. It is not unusual that people who take their own life are often remembered just for that reason and not for the other things that they have contributed during the course of their life.

There are many motivations for suicide, some that may come totally unexpectedly, some during mental illness, some during relentless periods of physical or emotional pain, which is felt by the whole family. People bereaved by suicide may feel that they are being punished. The question that is often asked is – why did he or she do this to me? What did I do to deserve it? Why has he or she abandoned me? Suicide challenges the value of life itself and places a question mark over the taboos against the taking of life.

Facts and figures

It is estimated that every two hours, someone in Great Britain commits suicide. In many countries, suicide is one of the ten leading causes of death. In 1988 official statistics demonstrated that around 4,300 people committed suicide in England and Wales during the course of that year. Many of those were people under the age of twenty-five. These statistics are based on coroners' verdicts and may not paint the accurate picture. Some coroners may be less inclined than others to pass verdicts of suicide because they would wish to seek protection for families from what is considered to be a distressing and unwelcome verdict which can often receive adverse and shocking publicity.

Child survivors of parental suicide

Given the difficulties many adults have in talking about death and in particular suicide, it is not surprising that children are often told little or nothing about how their parent died. Even when they are told something, information they receive may not be an accurate version of events. In view of the stigma that families feel, children are often told not to talk about the death and not to tell what they know.

Often children are sent away from home following suicide or are looked after by relatives or friends, not being given the opportunity to attend funerals or to find out what has really happened; often they piece the picture together by overhearing adult conversations. Adults, particularly parents, should be aware that children need to have honest and understandable information.

Michael's situation amplifies the problem that children often have to face when suicide happens. Michael was aged twelve when his father died. During counselling in his later life he described how he came home from school one afternoon to see an ambulance driving away from his house. He remembered a great deal of activity there and being met by an aunt who said that he and his younger sister were going to stay with her for a few days as his father was ill and his mother had had to go to hospital to be with him. It was not until the following day that he was told that his father had died of a heart attack. The next day he returned to school, but still staying with his aunt, and overheard some of his friends talking about the fact that they had heard that Michael's father had killed himself in the garage of Michael's home.

In bereavement counselling sessions years later he recounts his vivid memories of this time and the effect that this has had on his relationship with his mother, which prior to his father's death had been an extremely close and trusting one. He felt that to some degree he was helped by a teacher, not his own class teacher, who he now describes as not being able to cope with the situation. The teacher who came to his aid was somebody who had had a similar experience and allowed him to talk over his angry feelings and the particular sense of abandonment that he felt. He also talked of his great sense of isolation during the rest of his school life and the fact that his peers changed their attitude towards him. He talked of how teachers were insensitive to him, often talking about suicide in a throw away phrase and making jokes about dead people.

Michael, like many survivors of suicide, needed specialist help and teachers should be very aware of this when trying to assist children in school although they can do a great deal by being aware of the child's emotional pain, his guilt, angry feelings and the extreme sense of abandonment that a child who loses a parent by suicide inevitably feels.

Michael's experiences are not uncommon. Children are often sent away from home following a suicide and are looked after by distant relatives or neighbours. Often they are not even given the opportunity to attend funerals or to find out what has really happened. Like Michael, they often piece the picture together by overhearing other conversations. Many families just cannot cope with the stigma of having survived a suicide. They will often move house and change schools. As David Knapman has pointed out earlier, the need for a child's routine to be maintained is vitally important and a child who loses not only a parent but all their support systems at one time can feel devastated, which can have long term effects on the child.

Sibling survivors of suicide

Given the increasing incidence of suicide in the under twenty-five age group, it will not be an uncommon experience for some teachers to care for children whose brother or sister has committed suicide.

For the family, this may be the most devastating loss. For parents bereaved in this way it will be the overturning of all natural events and a halt to all their hopes and aspirations for their children's future. The fact that a child may have elected to die will leave some parents with the most tragic situation that they will ever have to face. It, therefore, follows that much of the attention will be focused on the parents and it may happen that siblings may be overlooked.

There is very little research that examines the effect on surviving brothers or sisters and there are few support services for siblings, although some organisations such as Cruse Bereavement Care and The Compassionate Friends are addressing this problem in some of their branches in the country.

For children losing a sibling through suicide there will be many powerful implications. As described earlier, children may be excluded from the activity that immediately follows the death. They may overhear adult conversations, may be excluded from attending the funeral and the veil of secrecy may prevail.

The child's grief processes may be determined very much by how the impact phase was dealt with, whether they were excluded, whether there are other siblings in the family – "Am I the only one left? Will I have to look after my parents?"

Most particularly, the quality of the relationship the child had with their dead brother or sister will have an effect on the grieving process. This can be a very important aspect especially if the relationship has been a difficult one. The bereaved child may feel an overwhelming sense of responsibility for what has happened, a feeling of being punished or of extreme guilt.

"I should have been nicer to him. I didn't mean to say horrible things to him". Jane, aged 8

Given that a child may be an overlooked mourner by his family, people in the child's normal routine and especially teachers, can play an important role in supporting a child bereaved in this way. The feelings of the child may be very profound, as earlier described, and they will need comfort and support.

A child aged fourteen whose brother recently committed suicide was frightened to return to school after his brother's death because he feared that his peers would make fun of him. His family approached the headmaster because of these fears and the headmaster dealt with the situation by talking to the child's peer group in a class situation and talking to them about death. This was very helpful in enabling the child to return to school and ultimately he was well supported.

Ways of helping children bereaved by suicide

It is likely that teachers will at some time during their career meet children who have either lost a parent or a sibling through suicide. The death is usually unexpected and shocking so not only will families be left with an endless list of questions surrounding the death, but teachers may feel immobilised and unable to know how to respond to children in their care. David Knapman suggests earlier in the chapter on bereavement that teachers can be in a key position to help bereaved children and do not necessarily need high-flown counselling skills. In the case of suicide, they do need to have an ability to recognise that often family members will not be honest with children. Teachers may be in a position to pick up warning signs and to inform parents or carers of any unusual behaviour that the bereaved child may be exhibiting. It is important to recognise the child will have very profound feelings, again identified in the chapter on bereavement, some of which, particularly anger, guilt and a sense of abandonment, may be heightened. The teacher too, may feel overwhelmed by what has happened and should, if needed, get help and support from professional colleagues.

Remember that children bereaved by suicide will be shocked and have difficulty in believing the death has really happened. If parents have tried to protect their children by leaving them out of the discussions and rituals the child can be left feeling anxious, bewildered, alone, punished and abandoned.

The child will be greatly helped by maintaining normal routines and it is important for teachers to provide an environment where children can be encouraged to talk about the death and express their feelings in a trusting way. It is important to talk to children in a language they understand and to listen to the child. If they are finding it difficult to express verbally their feelings, look at ways of helping them through play, drawing or painting. Focusing on feelings around the sense of abandonment and guilt may be helpful. Some children have found it particularly helpful to relate to one member of staff who they trust and who is able to set aside time for the child on a regular basis.

It is important for teachers to maintain good links with the family and give adequate feedback to parents about difficulties that might arise as far as the child is concerned.

It is important for the teacher to remember that it can take a long time to work through grief and that it is very normal for a child to express the same powerful feelings as an adult. If the child's reaction and behaviour worries teaching staff, then it is very important to seek advice from professionals. Educational psychologists, clinical psychologists and social workers may have much experience in helping children who have been bereaved by suicide and can be very helpful in assisting children and supporting staff.

Anna

Anna Dinnage lives in Devon and was ten when her nineteen year old brother Jon died suddenly and in tragic circumstances in July 1991. For Anna, her parents and her older brother Simon, this was the most devastating loss.

Anna not only had to cope with Jon's death but with a change from her primary school to the local comprehensive school just a few weeks after Jon's death. Both Jon and Simon attended the same school some years previously.

Anna is a remarkable person who has coped amazingly well with the loss of Jon and the way his loss has affected everyone in the family. She has had times at school when it has been hard, especially when death has been mentioned or when someone makes a throw away remark.

A teacher whom Anna trusts has been very supportive in making herself available when Anna has needed to talk.

The poems that follow were written by Anna. She, like other bereaved children, has found writing poetry helpful in expressing her grief.

Feelings

Never dreamt of anything so vile,
So much anger deep inside
And so far, many a mile,
In connection with everything.

Never thought it would come to this,
Sorrow and churning of whirling of thoughts.
Now I think, now I hope he's got what he wanted,
Utter bliss.

Myself

I stand and gaze, into a mirror and see
A small human shell child that is meant to be me!

If I was the creator, and made everyone,
Yes I'd make me like me, and on the Earth we'd live on.

This body of a robot has nothing to do with me!
Somebody made my soul inside that is full of laughter –
my personality.

When we move on, to our new heaven home
We leave our bodies and take our souls on their own

So don't cry for me, we still hold the dreams of
yesterday,
And the memories will all soon unfold.

References

Downey A 1987 *Dear Stephen* – a letter diary written to Stephen by his
    mother. Arthur James
Heegaard M 1988 *When someone very special dies*. Woodland Press
Parkes C M 1986 *Bereavement: studies in grief in adult life*. Routledge
Pincus L 1976 *Death and the family. The importance of mourning*. Faber &
    Faber
Rapheal B 1985 *The anatomy of bereavement*. Hutchinson
Wertheimer A 1991 *A special star*. Routledge

Useful organisations

The Compassionate Friends
53 North Street, Bristol BS3 1EW. Tel. 0272 539639

Cruse Bereavement Care
Cruse House, 126 Sheen Road, Richmond, Surrey TW9 1UR. Tel 081 940
    4818.

The Samaritans (Central Office)
17 Uxbridge Road, Slough, Berkshire SL1 1SN. Tel 0753 32713.

9 Children bereaved by violent death

For several years Dora Black, Consultant in Child and Adolescent Psychiatry at the Royal Free Hospital, and her colleagues Jean Harris Hendriks and Tony Kaplan, have been studying a series of children bereaved by the death of one parent at the hands of the other (Black et al 1991). We have now seen, personally, more than a hundred such children, of whom 90 percent have lost their mother at the hands of their father. Initially, referrals arose because of the interest of one of us (DB) in bereavement, others followed because we have a developing knowledge of legal issues concerning children and adolescents. Often, we have been asked for advice about where bereaved children should live, whether they should have access to the father in prison and about issues regarding compensation. We have become familiar with a growing literature on the effects of disasters upon children and the hitherto unrecognised high incident of post traumatic stress disorder which follows such disasters.

These children represent but the tip of an iceberg of those who witness violence, including sexual assaults, in their own home. From careful study of our cohort of children we hope to throw light on this wider field of unrelieved, indeed often unrecognised, domestic suffering and, by considering in particular the links between post traumatic stress disorder and mourning, to illuminate the suffering of children bereaved by other forms of violent death, for example those who witness the killing of their parent through other criminal violence, terrorism or war.

We hope that the stories of a few children, and the references on which we have drawn in trying to understand their suffering, will be of help to professionals faced with the needs of any child bereaved by violent death. This chapter stresses man-made violence because there is research evidence that disasters perceived as created by one's fellow men cause the greatest distress.

The children's stories

Mark and Anna:

A characteristic tale, not based on an individual child but on many tragedies described to us, might be that of Mark and Anna aged six and four years old. On the evening of his birthday Mark ran from the house to neighbours. He was incoherent. When they went with him to find out what was the matter the neighbours found Mark and Anna's mother dead from strangulation.

The children were referred for a psychiatric opinion two months after their mother's death. By now they were living in the same village, with close friends of their mother. Their father had been arrested soon after his wife's death and currently was in prison on remand. On the advice of his solicitor he was prepared to plead guilty to manslaughter. Also through his solicitor, he wished to arrange that the two children move to the home of his widowed mother until such time as he could resume their care.

The children's maternal grandparents were grateful for a plan, made by social workers called in at the time of the killing, that the family where the children were living would offer them a permanent home. They were friends of the children's mother who had offered emergency help and now wanted to care for her children as they felt she would have wished.

We were asked for an opinion as to whether the children should go to see their father in prison, and if it would be better if they stayed with their mother's friends, so that they could have frequent contact with the grandparents and other relatives on that side of the family, or whether father's plan, that the children should move a distance to his mother, might be better for them. There were concerns about how difficult it would be for the children to remain in the village where their mother had died and to continue at the same school.

We began by finding out what was the children's understanding of the crisis in their lives. We were told that the children were quite exceptionally easy to look after, very sweet tempered, good and well behaved and that they'd continued at the same school where everyone took great care not to talk with them about anything that had happened, not wanting to upset them. The family who wanted to care for the children long-term likewise were taking the greatest care not to upset the children nor to say anything that might remind them of their recent past.

John and Jane

John and Jane were nine and ten years old when their father battered their mother to death. Afterwards, he threw himself in front of a car and, at the time when we met the children, the father was in a surgical ward on traction, was expected to survive and was facing charges of murder.

The children had been moved 200 miles to the home of their mother's sister who had two young children of her own.

What happens next

When children lose one parent at the hands of the other, in effect they lose both. Usually also they lose access to their home, toys, possessions and school work, since commonly the home is occupied by police. The children may be the only source of information about the killing, about relatives who may be available to take care of them and about family life before the disaster which has overtaken them.

Commonly these crimes are committed in front of the children at the home, in its locality or among relatives. Often, they take place on significant family occasions such as contact visits after the parents have divorced or separated or on anniversaries such as birthdays, Christmas, New Year and other religious festivals. All routines familiar to the children disappear there and then and they become as flotsam in the wake of the investigations which follow. It is very rarely that they sleep in the parental home on the night of the killing except on occasions when the death has been concealed, as sometimes happens, and is not detected for an interval of time.

These children are invisible. When we began our project we realised that Home Office records of those convicted of murder and manslaughter give no information about the children. Psychiatrists and other specialists who assess the killer consider such issues as his or her fitness to plead, the concept of diminished responsibility and the prognostication as to whether there is risk of further violent crime. Probation services do take account of the families of criminals and alleged criminals but are under-resourced and do not have records that would enable identification of child victims of family crime. Many of the children in our study were unknown to departments of social services.

But these crimes are not uncommon. Home Office statistics on domestic homicide indicate that between 1982 and 1988, in cases involving a spouse, cohabitee or lover, a total of 164 women were charged with murder and thirteen with manslaughter and during the same period 753 men were charged with murder and thirty-two with manslaughter. The majority of these crimes are committed in domestic settings and involve women of child bearing age. The number of children who see their mother or father killed by other forms of violence is unknown.

Post traumatic stress disorder

It is necessary to think first about this concept because children who are traumatised cannot get on with grieving and if they cannot grieve their ability to retain or form trusting relationships becomes impaired. We have drawn on the work of Pynoos and his colleagues (1984, 1986, 1987 and 1988). Their American studies consider a range of violence witnessed by children and its effects upon them. Terr (1979 and 1981) has studied children on a school trip who were kidnapped, terrorised and abandoned in a school bus buried underground. Terr (1991) has written an invaluable outline and overview of the concept of trauma in childhood.

In the United Kingdom, Parry-Jones (1990) and his colleagues are studying the effects upon children of the disaster in which a Pan Am jet fell upon the town of Lockerbie in December 1988. Yule and his colleagues (1990 a & b) have studied the effects upon children of the sinking in 1987 of the Herald of Free Enterprise ferry boat off Zeebrugge in Belgium and the disaster in October 1988 when a boat containing adolescent school children sank in the Mediterranean with major risk to life and overwhelming, justifiable fear.

All of this work is recommended in particular to teachers, since the bulk of it refers to school children and in part assesses the effects of disaster upon children in school settings.

Post traumatic stress disorder (PTSD) is defined, in the revised diagnostic and statistical manual of the American Psychiatric Association (AMA 1987), as follows:

1 Existence of a recognised stressor which would evoke significant symptoms of stress in almost anyone.
2. Re-experiencing of the trauma indicated by at least one of the following:
    a) Recurrent and intrusive recollections of the event
    b) Recurring dreams of the event
    c) Suddenly acting or feeling as if the traumatic event were recurring because of association with an environmental or an ideational stimulus.

3. Numbing of responsiveness to or reduced involvement with the external world, beginning some time after the trauma, as shown by at least one of the following:

   a) Markedly diminished interest in one or more significant activities
   b) Feelings of detachment or estrangement from others
   c) Constricted effect.

4. At least two of the following symptoms which were not present before the trauma:

   a) Hyper-alertness or exaggerated startle response
   b) Sleep disturbance
   c) Guilt about surviving when others have not or about behaviour required for survival
   d) Memory impairment or trouble concentrating
   e) Avoidance of activities which arouse recollection of a traumatic event
   f) Intensification of symptoms by exposure to events that symbolise or resemble the traumatic event. (See Saigh (1988) for a discussion of the validity of DSM III 1980 in relation to children.)

The revised version of the manual allows diagnosis of PTSD only after an interval of twenty-eight days from the traumatic event.

Post traumatic stress disorder in childhood

The concept has been worked out by talking directly to children. What all the disaster work listed above has in common, and our research with children who have undergone private domestic violence confirms, is that the concerned adults, parents, other caretakers, social workers, teachers, doctors, lawyers, do not understand that the children are going through what adults also suffer because nobody can bear to talk to the children about it.

Take Mark and Anna; although both of them had been in the house at the time when their mother was killed, strangled by their father, no-one knew what they had seen or heard because no one had asked them. Not even Mark, who had run out of the house wordless and tearful, had been given any opportunity to tell what he had experienced. When asked to draw a picture about that night, he was able to do this and to describe the scene in vivid action replay. It was much later, in the course of therapy, that Mark began to weep for his mother and to express his horror and rage that he had not been able to protect her. Anna's two most horrible memories were that 'mummy swallowed her tongue' and of the smell which resulted from her dying mother's involuntary evacuation of the bowel. Anna's habitual constipation since the death suddenly had a meaning as indeed did her repeated drawings of rainbows consisting only of the colour red.

Anna and Mark had acquired some of their personal clothes and toys but photographs and other possessions were still in the family home. The paternal grandmother retained the key of his home and it was locked up pending a decision as to where the children would live. Anna and Mark were still in the legal guardianship of their father for several months after his imprisonment.

Principles for practice

We have begun to formulate these from the work which we have undertaken and from what the children have taught us.

1. We think that where children have been bereaved by violence within the family, and where as a result their legal guardian is in prison, accused of a major crime, **the state should act as parent.** We preferred the former arrangement of wardship which now alas is not available to local authorities. However, in England and Wales care proceedings within the framework of the Children Act 1989 may prove effective, providing these are regarded as cases so serious that they require the skills and knowledge of a higher court. The first need is for emergency care of the children. As much as possible should be done to obtain familiar toys and possessions. We understand that it is commonly the case that police must have access to the parental home for evidential reasons, but cannot think it necessary that children should be deprived of immediate necessities. It is important also that their toys, possessions and school work are not withheld from them in the course of battles between the two sides of their family. Where possible, it may be right that close relatives should care for the children in the emergency but it should be remembered that whether the children are placed with father's kin or mother's kin, may have far reaching effects upon what they learn of the killing and which relatives remain available to them. Almost inevitably there is conflict between father's and mother's families. Moreover,

relatives who become parents by default (Brinich 1989) are themselves grieving, possibly traumatised and with competing emotional and financial demands upon them. For example, John and Jane, when moved 200 miles to their mother's sister, were in the care of a parent who herself was overcome with grief and rage at the untimely death and was pregnant and the parent of two children under the age of five. She and her husband received no financial help with this new burden and indeed, for more than a year, were unable to get access to the children's home. Their father's father retained the key and refused all access since his hope and expectation was that his son would be found not guilty and would resume his own parental task.

Emergency placements should not become permanent by default.

2.　We have learned from disaster research that **these children require debriefing.** Of thirty children whom we have seen who were known to have witnessed the killing, twenty-seven had post trumatic stress disorder. Two were referred to us within three days of the killing and were debriefed; we think that this helped reduce the symptoms of traumatic stress. Retrospective histories indicate that many other children suffered nightmares, constricted effect, guilt at surviving where others had not and all the other symptoms listed above but that these were not recognised or identified at the time of the disaster.

The most important hurdle, to repeat, is the extreme unwillingness of all concerned further to upset the children. What happens is that the children become compliant and detached, their numbness is rather a relief to adults who are themselves grieving, angry and bewildered and no one finds out what is going on. We have talked with children who suffer the most horrendous nightmares unknown to those who care for them.

Their schooling is affected too. Yule et al (1990) describe how the girls on the Jupiter, the ship which sank in the Mediterranean, who were on average fourteen years old at the time of the disaster, showed a marked deficit in school performance during the two years up to the GCSE. They had been well above average at the time of the disaster and 'plummeted to near average'. These bright girls were still functioning in an acceptable way and it was not recognised that they were falling well below their own potential.

3.　**Children must be allowed to grieve.** We draw on the work of Lansdown and Benjamin (1985) on the development of the concept of death in children. The main task, particularly with

younger children, is to support the adults and to help them bear
the children's grief and to allow them to share family processes of
mourning. Often, we are asked to advise on whether children
should see the body – this reality may be as helpful to a child as to
the adults in facilitating mourning (Cathcart 1988), and whether
they should attend the funeral or some comparable ceremony
(Weller et al 1988).

4.   Children who have seen violent death **should be assessed** by
an experienced child mental health service **for evaluation of the
presence or absence of post traumatic stress disorder** and other
associated conditions such as absent or pathological mourning and
chronic anxiety states. Yule et al (1990 and 1991) show that further
anxieties may develop which are specific to the disaster undergone
by a particular child. Critical incident stress debriefing (Mitchell
1983, Pynoos 1986) must be complemented by careful support for
caretakers and professionals. Children who have seen the muti-
lated body of a parent are not helped by a refusal to recognise this
reality nor by a failure to allow them opportunities to speak of the
physical effects of disaster, their helplessness, their anger and their
grief.

5.   **Compensation claims:** in the United Kingdom children are
eligible for compensation from the Criminal Injuries Compensation Board (CICB 1989) for the death of a parent by criminal
violence. They may also sue the killer. Claims may also be made
on behalf of the children by those with parental responsibility
which may include a Department of Social Services or the official
solicitor acting on behalf of a ward of court, and the children may
claim on their own behalf within a period of three years
subsequent to their majority.

Careful record keeping, by doctors, social workers and teachers,
is essential for the effective pursuance of such claims. There may
be disputes also over insurance and policies and other family
properties, and legal representation of the children is often
necessary.

6.   Emergency placement must be followed by **careful urgent
planning** on behalf of the children who require legal representation for this reason also. The advantages and disadvantages of
placement with relatives must be weighed up with great care: in
particular, it is not appropriate to delay such decisions because a
criminal case against the father is not yet decided. In our experience the least successful placements so far have been those with
the father's kin, particularly if such relatives regard themselves
simply as keeping the child for the father until such time as his
release from prison. We are beginning to uncover evidence of the

most severe conflicts which can arise in situations such as this. It will be many years before we can gain adequate data about what the long-term outcome for children bereaved in this way may be (though we are beginning to get some painful stories from adults who, having heard of our work, have told us of their experiences after similar loss in childhood). In our view, it will be best that the state remains available as parent and legal guardian to children in this dilemma since their difficulties are neither short-term nor circumscribed.

School intervention

Firstly, we think it right that teachers should indeed be told about such tragedies in the lives of children. This may seem like common sense but we have known of cases where families have been so anxious to protect children that, after changes of school and domicile, attempts have been made to conceal all evidence of the past from health and educational services in the new setting. More usually, however, the teachers do know, but often they are assured that the children are doing remarkably well, which may not be true at all.

They are likely to come to school after disturbed sleep and to be suffering fears of the dark and of being alone. Usually, it is just as they are falling asleep, during that quiet time, that flashbacks and intrusive memories of the disaster occur. The children of Zeebrugge advise the use of music, just as they are going to sleep, to help divert frightening thoughts at this crucial time.

They are likely to be having great difficulty in separating from whoever is looking after them. They may be clinging and demanding in ways which appear, quite suddenly, much younger than their years. This behaviour is particularly difficult when the person to whom they are mainly attached, their mother, is the one who has disappeared. The substitute parents, themselves heavily burdened, will find this clinging most difficult.

Children do show changes in cognitive performance and at least on occasion, as with the Jupiter children, this is now documented. There is a difference however between a disaster like this which affects a substantial minority of a school population and that which affects just one or two children, perhaps siblings in two different classes. The simplest advice is to recognise, as a starting point, that children bereaved by domestic violence are not all right. If they are behaving as though nothing had happened, this is a problem. If they are bright and carry on acceptably within the middle of the range, this may be a considerable drop below what they are capable of achieving. They may be seriously impaired in their ability to trust others and to make reliable relationships. Children have trouble with remembering and sometimes may lose recently acquired skills such as the beginnings of computer studies or notation.

In school, many children show poor concentration. Intrusive thoughts are likely to occur at quiet times in the classroom just as they occur before sleep. The children may think they are going crazy. I worked with one girl, the subject of multiple rape, who was terrified by her visions of the attack, many of which occurred in school, and who was vastly relieved simply by being offered a clinical account of post traumatic stress disorder. This both relieved her fear that she was not schizophrenic and provided a comprehensible framework in which she could begin to under-stand the disaster which she had undergone. She'd been in a lot of trouble at school for poor work and this was not the fault of her teachers: they knew nothing of the rape. This girl was bereaved too, she could no longer live with her family.

Children suffering from personal, man-made violence are well aware of the stigma of having a crime in their family and that the adults around them also are very upset. The reluctance to talk is two-way, since the children do not want to upset the adults.

They are also isolated because they have not got any peers with whom to talk over their disaster. At least those in communal disasters like Jupiter, Lockerbie and the bus kidnapping, went through this with other children. Others are alone. They may be physically separated from their former school mates and emotion-ally they feel a great gulf.

They are much on the alert to danger too, just as are those who have been through public disasters. Opening the front door, going to the bathroom, walking down a particular street, may be the subject of the most intense fears which as indicated by Yule (1990) may lead to the development of quite clear cut, persistent and very specific phobic anxieties.

In summary, therefore, teachers should be on the alert when children have been violently bereaved. The children will be traumatised, probably having difficulty in grieving, dislocated, stigmatised and in the care of adults who are likely themselves to be suffering from very similar trauma or, if no family members are available, they may be in the care of strangers. Teachers may be told nothing at all or a bare outline of what has happened or may be given quite unrealistically rosy pictures of the children's adaptability and resilience. Children in disaster show fairly consistent responses as indicated by a range of research in clinical work during the last few years. Teachers who know about this work will be sensitive to disaster as it affects their pupils and their families.

References

American Psychiatric Association 1987 *Diagnostic and statistical manual of mental disorders* DMS R 3rd edn. Washington DC

Black D. Kaplan T. Harris Hendriks J 1991 Father kills mother: effects on the children In Wilson J. Raphael B. *The international handbook of stress.* Plenum Press, New York

Brinich P M 1989 Love and Anger in Relatives who 'adopt' Orphaned Children; Parents by Default, *Bereavement Care* 8(2): 14-16

Cathcart F 1988 Seeing the Body After Death, *British Medical Journal* 297, 997-8.

Criminal Injuries Compensation for children. 1989 Criminal Injuries Compensation Board. London & Glasgow

Lansdown R. Benjamin G 1985 The Development of the Concept of Death in Children aged 5 – 9. *Child Care Health Education* 11: 3-201

Mitchell J 1983 The critical incident stress debriefing process. *Journal of Emergency Medical Services* 36: 9

Parry-Jones W 1990 *Post disaster morbidity in children and adolescents. Identification and diagnosis.* University of Glasgow

Pynoos R S 1986 Witness to violence: the child interview. *Journal American Academy of Child Psychiatry* 25(3): 306-19

Pynoos R S. Frederick C. Nader K 1987 Life threat and post traumatic stress in school age children *Archives of General Psychiatry* 44: 1057-56

Pynoos R S. Nader K 1988 Psychological first aid and treatment approaches to children exposed to community violence. Research implicators, *Journal of Traumatic Stress* 1(4): 445-73

Terr L 1979 The children of Chowchilla: a study of psychic trauma *Psychoanalytic Study of the Child* 34: 547-623

Terr L 1981 Psychic trauma in children: observations following the Chowchilla bus kidnapping *American Journal of Psychiatry* 138: 14-19

Terr L 1991 Childhood traumas: an outline and overview *American Journal of Psychiatry* 148: 10-20

Weller E B. Weller R A. Fristad M A. Cain S E. Bowes J M 1988 Should children attend their parent's funeral? *Journal American Academy Psychiatry* 17(5): 559-62

Yule W. Williams R M 1990 Post traumatic stress reactions in children *Journal of Traumatic Stress* 2: 279-95

Yule W. Udin O. Murdoch K 1990 The Jupiter sinking: effects on children's fears, depression and anxiety *Journal of Child Psychology and Psychiatry* 31(7): 1051-61

10 Alcohol

Mixed messages

It would seem that almost from the beginning of time alcohol has played a considerable role in our social culture. From the discovery of rotting fruit to the mass manufacture of designer beverages, alcohol has accompanied our anthropological development. Along the way it has created many moral, religious and social dilemmas and today's society reflects very diverse attitudes and regard for its potential. Our apparent cultural views on the drug have become very confusing not least to our young people. Whilst one government department promotes healthy lifestyles and sensible drinking, another generates immense revenue through taxing our alcohol consumption. This ironically then helps to finance the phenomenal costs incurred through alcohol related illness, accidents and crime. For the 'respectable social drinker' alcohol is seen to project status and image, whilst someone who admits to a drink problem is often perceived to be the unrealistic stereotype, down and out, on a park bench. As adults, parents and teachers we often voice mixed messages about drinking by saying one thing and doing another. Despite our incongruity, statistics show that the majority of us are able to enjoy a drink and use alcohol sensibly, but if we do not understand or respect it for what it is, the consequences may be quite destructive.

There are infinite reasons as to why people drink and it is important to remember that alcohol problems seldom emerge in isolation and are often caused or compounded by other factors. Before any of us can even begin to unravel the strands of any alcohol 'tangle' it is imperative that we have first considered our own attitudes and feelings towards the drug, and recognise that there are no clear cut definitives or prescriptive solutions whether the person we are trying to help has the problem or is on the end of someone else's! When it comes to helping children it is sadly inevitable that they fall into both these categories.

Children and their drinking

The amount of research into the use of alcohol by children is limited and in the main focuses on those over the age of eleven. However, the research available indicates certain trends in children's drinking patterns. It is abundantly obvious that children are now drinking at a much earlier age (many beginning long before they reach eleven). We know that the highest percentage of alcohol consumed by children is obtained from the home and that the usual places for purchasing drink are surprisingly pubs, off-licences and clubs. On average boys are marginally more likely to drink than girls and the chances of either sex drinking accelerates between the ages of eleven and sixteen. Most children begin with either shandy or beer and lager with only a small percentage at first consuming spirits.

For some, by their drinking they are simply adopting what they perceive to be the norm, conditioned by parental or family behaviour, reinforced by the influence of the media and advertising and accepted as appropriate by their peers. Alcohol is socially acceptable and seldom regarded as a drug carrying comparable risks to other drugs, and because of this its use is often regarded as a normal factor in adolescence and a phase which will be outgrown. In some cases it would seem that John Balding's statement 'we teach them how to drink' is very apt. With such strong indicators it is difficult for some youngsters to envisage the use of alcohol as anything other than normal and expected, but perhaps for others their reasons are different. For some it may be the sheer thrill and excitement of risk taking, defiance or experimentation that dares them to defy any reasoning or apprehension, that stimulates their interest in alcohol. Yet for others it is quite possible that they drink simply because they like it and get something from it (after all, all drinking is functional whether it quenches the thirst, kills the pain or helps us to forget). Perhaps, however, the biggest factor common to young people's drinking is boredom. We now live in a fast moving world where expectations are high and success is clearly measured in materialistic terms and constant opportunities to enjoy new experiences. When those unrealistic prospects are not forthcoming youngsters often perceive that they are bored and that there is nothing else to do except congregate and drink, with alcohol becoming an increasingly important part of their sub-culture. For a minority of children, drinking will become the crutch they adopt to enable them to cope with the stress and pressure of their circumstances, convinced in their isolation that nothing or no one else can help. It is both sad and alarming to think that for some these are the launch-pads into adulthood and the role models that younger children may admire.

I am convinced that it is only through education and early intervention that we can hope to change attitudes and behaviour patterns for the future. Providing information and raising awareness of alcohol and its effects may help children to make informed sensible decisions about their drinking but this cannot be taught in isolation. It needs to be incorporated into an holistic approach that builds on self esteem, value and confidence in the individual. Recognition that children do drink and early identification of the symptoms may enable some children to be helped. Therefore it would appear that the teacher has two roles in alcohol policy – prevention and intervention.

Voices are often heard alerting us to the dangers of misusing alcohol; almost everyone is now aware of the risks of drink driving and the messages about health damage and social consequences are beginning to seep through. Children are at a far greater risk from the effects of alcohol than the average adult, and although we advocate sensible drinking levels (twenty-one units a week for men, fourteen units a week for women) they are not applicable to children or adolescents, and when we are highlighting the risks to children we need to emphasise some of the following:

- Alcohol is a poison to the human body, we need to slowly build up a tolerance to be able to cope with it;
- Young bodies and organs are still growing and developing and are very vulnerable to the damaging effects of alcohol;
- Children's bodies are physically smaller, lighter and fitter and the effects of alcohol are much stronger;
- Young people often drink in informal settings and do not appreciate the dangers of mixing drinks and unmeasured quantities;
- Alcohol is a depressant drug that 'closes down' the central nervous system. Children are at greater risk of passing out or of the respiratory system closing down resulting in death. Other children may not realise that once someone has passed out, their body continues to absorb the alcohol in their system putting them at tremendous risk if their friends do not know what to do;
- On average 1500 children a year find themselves in intensive care through alcohol. This does not include those admitted just to have their stomachs pumped out.

The need to finance any drug use including alcohol requires money and for some youngsters this means theft and petty crime which in turn can generate numerous other problems. This may be one of the first indications that someone is drinking. Apart from the obvious signs such as the smell of alcohol on the breath, empty bottles and cans, the features which may lead us to suspect a child is drinking are wide and varied. They include:

- erratic mood swings
- low self esteem
- anxiety and depression
- regular absence from school
- deterioration in performance
- apathy and lethargy
- over sensitivity to criticism or defensive attitude
- poor relationships with fellow pupils or staff
- persistent stomach upsets and headaches
- shakes
- attention seeking in an attempt to get help
- direct request for help.

Any teacher or parent glancing through this list would instantly realise that many of these symptoms could equally be attributed to other childhood problems and that it would be easy to draw the wrong conclusions. Every case will be different and the problem may manifest itself in the most unexpected ways that may bewilder or even defeat those who try to make sense of it. Perhaps the key to understanding and the invitation to help lies in building trusting relationships between pupils, teachers and parents, that can bridge the barriers of fear, denial and interference, creating an environment that assures confidentiality, non judgemental acceptance and empathetic support. I appreciate that this sounds wonderful in theory but is a tall order in reality. This is perhaps where the role of an alcohol policy comes into play. In the past alcohol problems in schools have been dealt with by suspension or expulsion, maybe in the hope that they would disappear.

A school policy has benefits for everyone. It offers clarity and direction as well as an agreed plan of action to resolve situations that may arise. Through negotiations and consultation it encourages governors, teachers and parents to lead by example. Through training it equips staff with basic skills in identification, listening and moving children forward towards making change and in how to refer to local support agencies if necessary. It provides a structured procedure offering support to pupils in exchange for commitment and effort. It also provides parents with a better understanding of alcohol and also encourages them to explore the grey area of their children and drinking. Most of all it provides an on-going comprehensive education in alcohol awareness which above all will prevent problems arising in the first place. To be effective it needs to be established before situations arise and will need regular monitoring, reviewing and updating.

Bearing the brunt

It is a sad fact that children are often the ones who bear the brunt of adults' problems and when it comes to alcohol they have often been referred to as the fogotten casualties. In the main, support and therapy are aimed at the problem drinker and possibly including their partners, but it seems that few 'set ups' are equipped or have the capacity to answer the needs of the children. As a result, studies into the impact that problem drinkers have on their children are sparse and limited and consequently so is our insight into their world and how they cope. The number of children who catch our attention probably represents only a minority of all those affected by someone else's drinking. Perhaps this is because some youngsters are remarkably resilient and adaptable and find ways to overcome situations, perhaps in some instances solutions are found or some kind of balance is maintained by making adjustments in the family structure. For some, life will be difficult and painful. Again there are no set formulae to detect such children, although some of the symptoms they may display are akin to those exhibited by children who drink themselves and include delinquency, truancy, hyperactivity or the reverse, introversion. Along with their outward behaviour these forgotten victims also carry a mixed bag of feelings and emotions which may be difficult to express, share or even accept. Amongst them we often find:

confusion	loneliness
fear	isolation
mixed loyalties	helplessness
guilt	anger
embarrassment	anxiety
hurt	disappointment

It is an onerous and formidable list and one which would probably leave most of us feeling inadequate and possibly impotent, and we have not yet taken into account some of the other implications of a drinker in the family. Poor relationships, financial problems and imbalance of roles are just a few of the 'knock on effects' often experienced. Teachers cannot resolve family problems necessarily, but they can recognise some of the immediate needs of their pupils most of which are quite basic:

- to be believed
- to be listened to and heard
- to be brought out of their isolation and feel supported
- to offload
- to express and explore their feelings
- if they want to, to be assisted to get further help and support.

As adults we often underestimate the abilities of children to make decisions for themselves and to respect that sometimes they do know what is best in their situation. Teachers do not have the levels of expertise and knowledge to intervene in family situations nor to be expert counsellors in the alcohol field, but they can be alert, know their pupils and build trusting relationships with them, be informed, be available and feel confident to take the first steps towards helping and answering the immediate needs as well as knowing how to refer on if necessary to local support agencies. If a school is equipped with an alcohol policy most of these issues would be addressed in the training element and staff would feel prepared rather than helpless, inadequate, and out of their depth at suddenly being confronted by a child who is affected by someone else's drinking or the consequences of it.

Sources of help

There are two main sources who might put you in touch with any local support or counselling services or specific projects to assist such children:

AL-Ateen
61 Great Dover Street, London SE1 4YF

National Children's Home
Chief Office, 85 Highbury Park, London N51 1UD

11 The school student and drug use

Substances

Substances which have changed the way people think, feel or act, have been with us for thousands of years. These substances fall into four main categories.

1. **Stimulants** increase central nervous system functions, delay sleep, increase alertness, increase blood pressure, heart rate and temperature, suppress appetite, give feelings of confidence and increased ability. In higher doses they can cause anxiety, aggression and paranoia. As the drug is lost from the body these symptoms diminish and could be replaced by feelings of tiredness, irritability, depression and hunger.

   Examples of this category of drugs are Amphetamine, Cocaine, Crack, XTC, Caffeine and Nicotine.

2. **Depressants** decrease central nervous system function causing drowsiness, relaxation, relief from anxiety, impairment of mental and physical function, reduced sensitivity to pain, both physical and mental. In higher doses they cause stupor, unconsciousness, 'drunken' behaviour. Effects can be dangerously potentiated if two or more types of depressant are taken at the same time. Withdrawal effects may include flu-like illness, cramps, nausea, sweating, depression, loss of sleep pattern.

   Examples of these types of drug are barbiturates, tranquillisers, alcohol, opiates and their derivatives, namely morphine, heroin, codeine, methadone.

3. **Hallucinogens** change people's perception causing heightened sensory experiences, feelings of unreality or dissociation, mood elevation, awareness, occasionally panic and anxiety. True hallucinations are rare.

   LSD and Magic Mushrooms (psilocybin) are the most common of this group. XTC (MDMA) and analogues could also fit into this category. Rarely available Phencyclidine and Mescaline.

4. **Others**
    Cannabis can have the effects on the user of any of the other categories depending on the amount taken and the expectation of the user. It is the most widely used illicit substance.
    Solvents and gases. Many hundreds of brand products are available ranging from glues, lighter fuels, cleaning fluid, butane gas and aerosols containing fluorocarbons. Like cannabis, the effects on the user are subjective although chemically these substances are depressants on brain and central nervous system function.

There are many publications available that describe these drugs in more detail. I would recommend the Institute for the Study of Drug Dependence (ISDD) *Drug Abuse Briefing*.

Why might young people take drugs? A good question, and of course there is not one single answer but very likely a range of reasons. A study from 1988 concluded the main reason for young people starting to take drugs was curiosity – they had heard about drugs, read about them, seen television programmes, knew people who had or were taking them and, because of these influences, which included peer pressure, felt they wanted to try them too. Other reasons could be pleasure – the fact is that some of these drugs do produce enjoyable effects at least initially; self-medication – to escape from or relieve feelings of anxiety, frustration, depression, boredom or unhappiness; rebellion – against parents or authority, seeking attention and risk taking; lack of success, not just at school but in other areas of their lives; family background – they may come from a disturbed home and lack love and care, through divorce or other loss of parents; it may be that the parents themselves are drug users and the home attitude influences the child; availability – people use the drugs they have access to and can afford.

It is important not to focus solely on the drug use, which may be only a symptom of underlying problems, but to assess the whole life situation, as appropriate, of the user.

Drug use can be experimental; using on an occasional basis perhaps to find out the effects a substance will have. Some people do not like that experience and so stop or move away from drug taking. Others who do like the effects may move on to experiment with other drugs or move into recreational use. This is where the drug use is still controlled and frequently only used at weekends. The other category of drug use is dependence. Invariably, the substance is used on a daily basis, sometimes chaotically, often not for any 'pleasurable' effects but to stave off withdrawal symptoms.

It is not necessarily true that all recreational cannabis smokers go on to become dependent injectors of heroin.

How are drugs taken?

Orally – swallowed as pills, capsules or tablets, in liquid form, mixed with food, as a food additive or in its natural state. Absorption is through the stomach and small intestine into the bloodstream. This is a relatively slow and inefficient method as digestive juices destroy some of the drug and the presence of food in the stomach retards absorption, which can make it difficult to predict or control effects.
Nasally – drugs like amphetamine, cocaine and solvents sniffed or inhaled up the nose. There is rapid absorption through blood vessels lining the nose.
Smoking – smoke and fine particles are absorbed through the lungs into the bloodstream. Efficient and rapid effect.
Injection – which can be just under the skin, deeper into a muscle or into a vein. The intravenous route is the most effective as the drug enters directly into the bloodstream. However, this method also carries the most risks.

Identifying the drug user

This can be a most difficult task. As children grow into young adults they go through physical, hormonal, mental and behavioural changes that can be as confusing for them as they are for adults who observe them. The most obvious confirmation of drug use would be to catch someone in the act and therefore make denial difficult! The following list may give some other clues towards identifying drug use, but it would be for the teacher or parent to observe a suspected individual most carefully before making any judgement or accusation. Remember that some of these symptoms may indicate something else other than drugs:

Identifying the drug user:

Equipment	Physical	Mental	Behavioural
Small mirror	Injection	Personality and	Clock watching
Razor blade	Dilated constricted	emotional changes	Work deterioration
Short straws/tube	pupils	i.e. Aggressive,	Lateness
Syringe/needles	Reddened nostrils	Unpredictable,	Truancy
Small envelopes of	Sores around mouth	Apathetic,	Accidents
mag. paper	Loss of weight	Withdrawn,	Furtive behaviour
Tin foil	Ashen skin colour	Oversensitive,	Secretiveness
Burnt spoon	Alcohol-like	Unco-operative	Talkative
Acetic acid	intoxication	Confusion	Lack of emotion
Powders	Hangover	Lack of	Disassociation from
Long cigarette papers	Nausea/vomiting	concentration	surroundings and
Small home made	Sedation	Anxiety	reality
pipes	Lowered resistance	Depression	Changes in friends,
Vegetation	to infections	Phobias	dress and interests
Transfer covered	Disregard for	Delusions	Talking drug jargon
paper	physical	Persecution	and phrases
Various coloured/	appearance	paranoia	Less responsible
shaped tablets	Wearing sunglasses		Difficulties in
Solvent containers	(at inappropriate		communication
Crisp packets/plastic	times)		Lack of money
bags			Borrowing of money
Smells: Aftershave/			Crime
perfume			

A person who shows signs of: severe anxiety, tremors, shaking, flu-like symptoms, headaches, sweating, muscle pains, diarrhoea, vomiting, sleep disturbance, depression, hallucinations and general debility may have withdrawal difficulties. However, some people may show no outward signs of drug use.

The difficulties associated with drug taking

Drugs are never free: they always cost something, perhaps in terms of gaining or losing a reputation, money, loss of health, loss of freedom and time. The difficulties fall into three broad areas: legal, social and health. They are not necessarily separate from each other and quite frequently overlap.

Legal

As some of the drugs concerned, and some of the behaviours that stem from their use, are illegal, it seems reasonable to assume that sooner or later the user, their family or a school will come into contact with the law. It may be that the police visit the school to investigate suspicion or confirmed drug use, or to remove substances that may be drugs but as yet remain unidentified, or even to arrest.

The process, broadly, is that the police would interview the young person concerned with an adult present. The officer would make a report to his or her line manager at the police station who could then send a copy to the Crown Prosecution and to the multi agency juvenile panel (Youth Court Panel) who would discuss the case and recommend whether to prosecute or not. They may also recommend (1) no action, (2) advice only (to child and/or parents), (3) a formal caution, (4) prosecution, involving a court appearance and a report from Social Services or Probation, which may lead to a conviction. Penalties vary and are subject to the severity of the case which may well affect a young person's future should they be convicted, as convictions are recorded, and they may need to declare it on any job application. Attitudes towards drug users from prospective employers are not good and would make it extremely difficult to gain employment.

Social

It can be very difficult from a parent's point of view to be told that your child is a drug user. All sorts of emotions surface; anger, guilt, shame, confusion, sense of failure as a parent; but in some cases, apathy. Parents (and teachers) may struggle to communicate with a child over drug taking issues. If that difficulty arises then there can be two extremes: (1) ignore the situation, deny it, pretend it cannot happen in this family, or (2) be outraged by it and make accusations and threats. Neither extreme is at all helpful and only creates more barriers to overcome. The alienation caused may push a young person further into drug use. This alienation may extend into the circle of non drug using friends, which would then leave the drug user either isolated or further acquaintanced to the drug using culture.

How do drug users obtain their supplies? Money, of course, has purchasing power but non-working school age children with limited income may resort to theft from parents, home, shoplifting, opportunist burglary, prostitution or become drug dealers themselves, depending on the need of the individual including the cost of the drug.

Social costs could include community services and time, for

instance involvement of police, GPs, hospitals, probation, social services and so on.

Health

Health risk can be immediate, such as having an allergic reaction to a drug, or cumulative, namely a gradual breakdown of physical and mental function. No one can guarantee how they will be affected by a drug even if they have taken it before; there are many factors which need to be considered. The main ones are:

1. Has the drug been accurately identified? Street drugs are rarely pure. They are adulterated by other substances such as glucose powder, chalk, talcum powder, washing powder, brick dust, cocoa powder, chopped herbs, which means that the percentage of actual drug is usually very small. There are no quality controls or guarantees for street drugs.
2. Overdose – too much at one time or too often, but which can relate back to the quality of the drug.
3. Accidents – falls, cuts, bruises, burns, while under the influence of drugs.
4. Dependence – has already been mentioned earlier.
5. Drug injectors or those who do not practise safer sex can run the risk of contracting hepatitis or HIV/AIDS, besides unwanted sex or unwanted pregnancy. Injectors can have difficulty with their injecting sites: hot or cold abscesses, septicaemia, collapsed veins or blocked blood vessels.
6. Someone showing signs of acute anxiety, flu-like symptoms, shaking, sweating, headaches, nausea, diarrhoea, irritability or aggression and general debility may be experiencing withdrawal. These physical symptoms can be distressing and uncomfortable, but fortunately do not last for more than a few days or weeks. The psychological symptoms will take longer to overcome and invariably require some form of counselling

Some practical advice for school staff

It is important that school staff are thoroughly prepared and informed about drugs, and, should drug use occur in school, should have an agreed policy of procedures in existence to refer to, rather than wait and be caught unprepared and possibly make panic decisions whilst under pressure.

Devise (or review existing) school policy on drug use. This could include the school's definition of drug use and the procedures that members of staff will need to take to ensure the safety of the child and the integrity of themselves and the school, should individuals' drug use be discovered. It could take the form of a 'flow chart' an example of which is shown (Figure 1) taken from *Guidelines for the Management of Substance Related Problems and Incidents in the Secondary School* copyright Lancashire County Council (1989).

Staff training. All staff should have basic drug awareness training so they will know the signs, symptoms and effects of drug use. This will enable them to discuss in a non-judgemental way drug use and to give accurate information on the risks of that drug use. Training may also include basic and emergency first aid.

Education. Drug education and issues could be brought up under the headings of personal social development and health education: making people responsible for their own well being. Some sources have suggested that six or seven years old would not be too young to start this. However, I feel it would be unfair if the target group were solely young people. School governors, teaching staff, other school staff and parents themselves need to be offered the opportunities to raise their own awareness of drugs. An example of this awareness could be for the school to organise its own Health Week when the pupils devise their own poster, collect leaflets, invite in local drug agency staff, the Police Community Affairs Officer and HIV Prevention Co-ordinator. Parents' and teachers' workshops could be organised. Learning about oneself can be hard work, so it is essential to make that learning fun, even with such a potentially serious subject as drug use.

Learn about harm reduction. Basically this means reducing the risks being run, regardless of whether the use is experimental, recreational or dependent. It can be difficult to change behaviours, particularly if deeply entrenched. School staff should not expect immediate change in a drug using student. This very rarely happens overnight, but is more likely to occur over weeks, months, possibly years in some individuals.

Local drug services. Find out where they are, who they are, what they do. All of these services are confidential and it is easy to talk to them. Most of them have an information resource as well as running a counselling service for users. School staff should not feel isolated about dealing with drug issues, but build up a network of support services which can act in a consultative way and help schools make decisions.

Devise a pupil concern record sheet. This must be as confidential

Figure 1 A flowchart of school procedures in response to a substance related problem

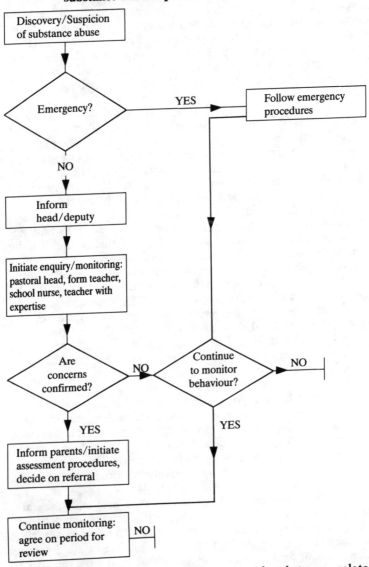

From: Guidelines for the management of substance related problems and incidents in the secondary school, Lancashire County Council 1989

as you can make it and it will enable you to note changes of attitude, behaviour, extreme mood swings, physical condition and performance which may indicate a leaning towards drug use.

If I had to encapsulate my advice to anyone who finds themselves confronted by suspected or confirmed drug use, I would use Clive Dunn's hackneyed phrase 'Don't panic!' as over-reaction all too often makes the situation worse. Instead, think about where help, advice and support can be found.

References and reading materials

ADFAM National (for the families and friends of drug users)
1st Floor, Chapel House, 18 Hatton Place, London EC1N 8ND Tel 071 4053923

Department of Health *Drugs – a parent's guide. Solvents – a parent's guide*
Healthwise
4th Floor, 10/12 James Street, Liverpool L2 7PQ Tel 051 2311266
Training packs: *Taking drugs seriously* and *Don't panic*
Institute for the study of drug dependence (ISDD)
1 Hatton Place, London EC1N 8ND Tel 071 4301991
Re-Solv: The Society for the prevention of solvent and volatile substance abuse
30a High Street, Stone, Staffordshire ST15 8AW Tel 0785 817885
Standing Conference on Drug Abuse (SCODA)
1/4 Hatton Place, London EC1N 8ND Tel 071 2312341
Teachers' Advisory Council on Alcohol and Drug Education (TACADE)
1 Hulm Place, The Crescent, Salford M5 4QA Tel 061 7458925
Tyler A *Street Drugs*

12 Groupwork with stressed children: Teaching children to be good friends

Introduction

This chapter is written by an educational psychologist who works a generic area patch across both a rural and an urban environment. It is in the nature of this type of work that one frequently comes across pupils who are experiencing difficulties in forming relationships within school, both with their peer group and with the adults who are entrusted to teach and support them. Pupils who are experiencing emotional and behavioural problems raise a high level of concern amongst teaching staff, not only because of the disruptive effect they can have on lessons, but also, in the case of the withdrawn, isolated or bullied pupil, because staff often feel that they are difficult to help.

Frequently, behaviour management programmes will have been advised and carefully followed by staff in school and whilst the programme has been in place they will have been found to be effective. Frustratingly, all too often, once the rigorous monitoring and positive feed-back is eased off, the problem re-emerges and staff are left feeling that their hard work has been merely a containment exercise and that the problems must therefore be within the child, or at least generated from the home situation, and therefore there is little that can be done in school. There is also the problem of the child who has low self-esteem and is withdrawn and isolated, perhaps caught in a web of learned helplessness. Something more than giving positive feedback appears to be required, as there is the danger that both teacher and pupil will feel that it lacks sincerity.

Parents, teachers and society in general persist in viewing behavioural issues in terms of motivation and not skills. It seems inconsistent to focus so closely on the consequences of behavioural difficulties when we do not do this with other forms of learning. It may be more appropriate to start by looking at what the child brings to a situation; whether the child has the necessary interactional skills and abilities needed in particular contexts. These factors can be identified by using an information processing model. It is also important to recognise that some of these skills may be thinking skills. Very often, pupils who present behavioural difficulties within school have a very restricted range of responses which leads them into conflict with both other pupils and adults.

One of the benefits of the new National Curriculum is the emphasis that it places on speaking and listening. This positively encourages schools to look at ways in which they can develop children's communication skills and there is a great emphasis within the National Curriculum on encouraging children to work co-operatively in groups (English Key Stage I Attainment Target I levels 1/2/3 Speaking and Listening; Science Attainment Target I levels 1 and 6).

Dunne and Bennett (1990) point out that the lack of demand for co-operation in typical clasroom groups shows itself in the quality of the talk in which children engage. 'The major weakness of current grouping practice seems to be that there is usually no specific demand on children to work together, and rarely is the group given the opportunity to work on a group task.'

Recent research on classroom groups has emphasised the need to direct children towards more co-operative ways of working in order to improve the quality of their performance. 'It is likely that pupils' performance could be substantially improved if they were given regular opportunities in the classroom to use their speaking and listening skills over a range of purposes in a relaxed atmosphere.' (From Assessment of Performance Unit, 1986)

The importance of developing the skills to interact with others successfully has also been an area of interest for workers involved in conflict management programmes, both in the UK (Saunders 1989, Montgomery 1986, KFWG 1987) and in the States (Prutzman et al 1978) over a number of years. Conflict management strategies emphasise the benefit of co-operation and communication in problem-solving and they stress the importance of encouraging individuals to value themselves as this will help them to respect and value the strengths of those around them. Increasingly, workers have recognised the long-term effects on an individuals' social and emotional wellbeing of being able to relate to one's peer group successfully.

In this chapter the author will describe how these ideas have been taken up in a number of the schools with which she works. This type of work can be particularly helpful with stressed children, as research has demonstrated the value of peer support and the benefits that the structured society of school can offer to a pupil whose life is going through a crisis. Appropriate coping strategies can be taught within the safe boundaries of such developmental groupwork. By describing in some detail one particular project, the author will attempt to address some of the issues which arise when setting up such interventions and evaluate the outcomes to date.

The Project

The author was approached by senior staff in one 500-pupil middle school in her patch who were expressing concern about the number of pupils in year seven presenting with emotional and behavioural problems.

The author has had some experience over a number of years working with abuse victims in small groups and also offering individual counselling, both to the victims of abuse and to children presenting in school with severe emotional and behavioural problems. Although in the author's experience disturbed pupils may respond well to positive behaviour management, a long-term generalisation to more effective peer and teacher relationships and interactions is rarely achieved, particularly at the secondary stage. The author was therefore keen to try an intervention which would offer a more lasting solution for pupils who had failed to establish good relationships and who were unable to cope with mainstream education without getting into staff/pupil conflicts. The request from the Middle School seemed to offer an opportunity to try an alternative approach.

It was suggested to the school that they might like to exchange the normal monthly time-allocated visits for fortnightly sessions which would use conflict management techniques and developmental groupwork to help these pupils improve their personal relationships and self-esteem. At the outset it was made clear that if the school opted for this type of intervention they would not have any individual child assessment work done during the period that the project was running. It was agreed that the project would be set up in two phases. Phase one would involve the author and a member of the school staff and phase two would involve the member of staff who had worked on phase one of the project and another member of the teaching staff. It was agreed that this would be a useful way of introducing conflict management strategies and ideas within the school.

The initial request was made during the summer term 1990 and phase one of the project started in the second half of the autumn term of that year.

Implementation

The project would never have got off the ground without the full support of the headteacher, although he had little direct contact with the running of the project. It was decided that the pupils' head of year seven would work as co-worker with the author on the project. Although the initial discussions had taken place with the head of special needs, the school's decision to co-opt a senior member of staff who was also the key stage leader to the project made an enormous difference to its impact within the school. Year seven tutors agreed to collect pre-project data and liaise with subject teachers over missed course work. These negotiations were delegated to the school and took place prior to the final agreement for the project to start.

The school also took on the responsibility of explaining to parents what was proposed and getting their agreement. However, as the initial target group of pupils were all the subject of a high level of concern in school already, with frequent parental contact the norm, selling a positive intervention to parents was not as problematic as it might otherwise have been. Once phase one had established the benefits for pupils of this type of intervention, it became easier to engage the support of staff and parents.

The group

During the first half of the autumn term the school were asked to decide which of the eighteen or so pupils they were concerned about were priorities for phase one. They were asked to decide on a group of between six and nine pupils. Teachers' perceptions of the severity of the behavioural and emotional difficulties were assessed by the completion of Bristol Social Adjustment Guide (BSAG) forms for each pupil. These were filled out by their tutors and the head of special needs. The final group decided upon for phase one consisted of seven boys and two girls. BSAG scores indicated that three of the group were showing severe maladjusted over-reaction; two moderately maladjusted over-reaction; three were showing maladjusted under-reaction ranging from appreciable to severe; and one was presenting with significant neurological signs. Four of the pupils were victims of known abuse, two of them had been the subject of sexual abuse. All the group members were reported by their teachers to have a low self-image and difficulties in relating to peers and staff in school, these concerns having been identified at initial referral and during on-going school-based assessments.

Timing

The timing of the sessions was largely dependent on the availability of the head of year. There were two or three possible options during the week. Unfortunately, there was no time when all tutor groups involved were occupied either on the same activity or on an activity that was deemed by all those involved to be of low priority. This was quite an issue as subjects such as PE, art and cookery were highly valued by group members but were considered by staff as suitable for alternative curriculum activities as they were not core subjects. The problems of competing activities were illustrated by the fact that the second of our meetings had to be abandoned due to a clash with inter-house rugby in which all the boys wanted to be involved. With hindsight, it might have been easier to use some of the core curriculum English time for the period of the project as part of the National Curriculum requirement for speaking and listening. 'By talking, discussing, arguing, planning, describing every day in school children become better at doing these things so that they have skills ready for the job interview, the workplace – and for sorting out the situations that family life often throws up.' (National Oracy Project 1989)

The theory

The project drew heavily on the framework for creative problem solving and conflict management developed by the Kingston Friends Workshop Group (KFWG).
  'Successful conflict resolution and good relationships are built on self-confidence and an absence of fear.' (*Ways and Means*, KFWG 1987).

This approach maintains that you can help children through various activities which enhance communication skills, increase their level of co-operation with other pupils and adults and raise the value they put on themselves and each other. In this way they will build up their self-confidence and this, in turn, leads to more effective problem-solving. There are three essential building blocks fundamental to creative problem solving, namely communication, co-operation and affirmation. The natural problem solver has these skills and uses them unconsciously. The skills themselves, however, can be illustrated, practised and improved by those who are experiencing difficulties with relationships. These are not new ideas and have broad appeal across the whole curriculum.

'In much of the best work the children undertake investigations in small groups. This helps them to develop their ability to co-operate, to communicate, to negotiate and to respect each other's views. In working together they also learn to share ideas and teach skills to each other.' (HMI Science Report 1989)

The activities in *Ways and Means* (KFWG 1987) are all designed to encourage discussion. It is through the managed interactions that follow from this discussion that pupils learn their new problem solving skills.

Creating a co-operative atmosphere

To develop an atmosphere in which the pupils could feel safe to work through negative or aggressive feelings required some careful consideration of the ground rules that would apply.

Numbers: The group needed to be small enough for all the group members to feel fully involved.

Identity: In the first session tasks were chosen which specifically reinforced individual group members' sense of identity and established personal contacts. The idea that group members are cherished as individuals irrespective of the views expressed about their behaviour on occasions is essential to this type of approach.

Agenda setting: Initially the activities were planned and decided upon by the author and the head of year, but as the group developed the areas to be worked on were increasingly agreed by the group as a whole. Demonstrating to the group members that they can negotiate to work on areas that they feel they need to develop is seen as an important skill area to promote, and one which not only enhances self-esteem and self-worth but also shows them that authority figures can listen to and value their ideas and needs. It also shows them that they can learn to present their ideas in ways which will get them a sympathetic hearing outside the nurturing environment of the group. A brief evaluation of each session was made by the author and the head of year (as co-workers) at the end of each session.

Avoiding raised voices: A signal for 'Quiet Please' was agreed at the initial meeting. Our group decided on a raised hand, palm front. As group members noticed someone making the sign they stopped speaking and made the sign themselves. Careful explanation and rehearsal at the outset ensured that this sign was very effective. It enabled any group member to establish communication with the group leaders or other children.

At the initial session the aims and objectives were outlined to the group members and we used the iceberg analogy described by the Kingston Friends Workshop Group (KFWG) in their handbook *Ways and Means*. This suggests that solving problems is only the tip of the iceberg with listening skills, self-expression, willingness and ability to work together, and positive self-awareness and affirmation of others being the underlying cognitions necessary for creative thinking. We also used the bridge-building analogy which suggests that relationships are under-pinned by understanding each other, helping each other and valuing each other. Every group member also had a copy of the simplified ground rules (see Figure 1).

Equipment

Apart from the initial session, any equipment needed for the workshop was specified on the workshop record, a copy of which was kept by both co-workers. The record would also specify who was to provide what for the session. The record was used for a brief post-session evaluation and formed a good basis for setting up the work to be done on the following session (see Figure 2).

Records

In addition to the records kept by the group leaders the pupils also kept an on-going record of what happened during the sessions, which included an evaluation of how they felt the sessions had gone. Some of our group members had literacy difficulties and it was therefore seen as important to allow them to record their feelings about the sessions pictorially, if they preferred (see Figures

WORKSHOP RECORD

Run by: _____   Date: _____

with: _____

Time: _____

Aim of Session: _____

Materials needed:

1 _____   5 _____

2 _____   6 _____

3 _____   7 _____

4 _____   8 _____

ACTIVITIES	BRIEF EVALUATION
1	
2	
3	
4	
5	

Evaluation of Session:

Figure 2 Workshop record

GROUND RULES

1. You do not have to take part in any activity that makes you feel uncomfortable *but* neither must you spoil activities which the rest of the group want to enjoy.

2. You are allowed to ask questions if you do not understand what to do.

3. This way of working is intended to help people to get on with each other better by teaching them to

   listen to each other
   understand each other
   value each other

4. Part of valuing each other is to listen to what other people say and not make fun of their contributions.

5. Quiet sign – when you notice someone making the quiet sign, make it yourself and be quiet and listen.

Figure 1   Ground Rules

EVENT NAME

ACTIVITY	YES	O.K.	NOT SURE	NO
1.				
	COMMENT			
2.				
	COMMENT			
3.				
	COMMENT			
4.				
	COMMENT			
5.				
	COMMENT			

ONE POSITIVE THING

ONE THING LEARNT

ONE THING ENJOYED

ANY OTHER COMMENT

Figure 3 Pictorial record (1)

THINGS WE DID

ACTIVITY			WHY DID WE DO IT?

WHICH DID YOU ENJOY MOST?

WHAT WAS THE MOST IMPORTANT THING YOU LEARNT?

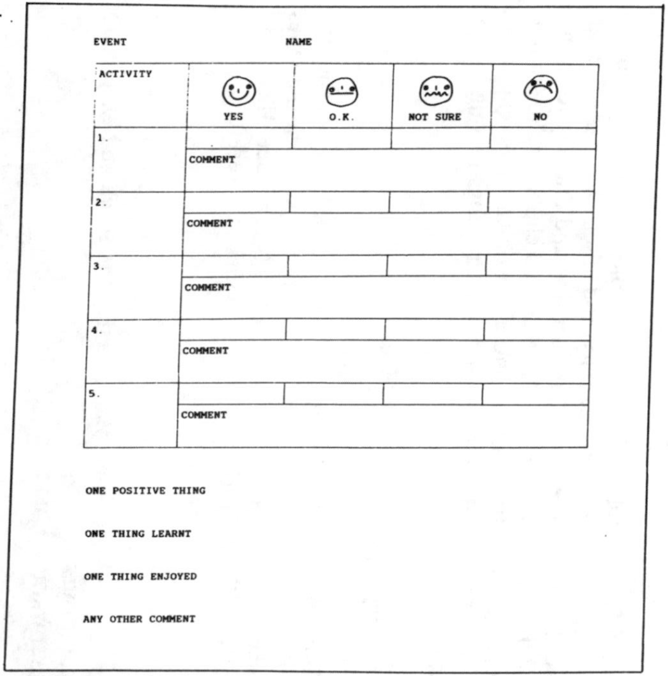

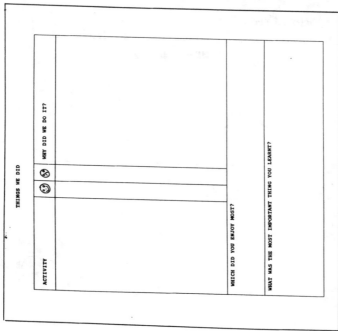

Figure 4 Pictorial record (2)

Figure 5 Pictorial record (3)

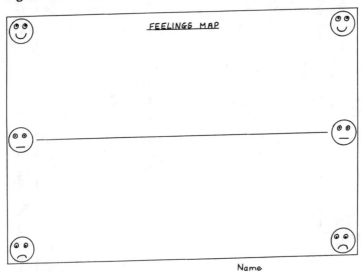

3, 4 and 5 for examples). However, despite the fact that most of the sessions were primarily activity and discussion based, much hard work went into recording and writing and drawing for group tasks. Pupils had made their own decorated clipboards to support work during the initial sessions and a plastic envelope clipped to each board prevented their writings and drawings getting lost or scruffy.

The workshops

For more detailed examples of workshop records and evaluation please refer to appendices at the end of this chapter. The activities used in each workshop are briefly listed below. See *Ways and Means* (KFWG 1987) for details of activities referred to.

Week one

Aim: getting to know each other, setting the scene and explaining the ground rules.
Activities: warm-up 'names'

- Names and affirming adjectives
- Labels and likes
- Clipboard logos
- Feelings maps

Week two

Aim: co-operative activities used to explore feelings towards each other and others.
Activities: warm-up 'paper-backs'
- Finish clipboards; rehearse ground rules
- Co-operative picture
- Feelings maps

Week three

Aim: enhance listening skills
Activities: warm-up 'quicklist – what makes a good listener?'
- Listening for feelings 'Support or Sabotage?'
  (Is hunting a great British tradition or cruel and out of date?)
- Discussion
- The Maligned Wolf story
- 'I' messages . . .

Week four

Aim: improving communication/co-operation
Activities: warm-up 'zoom'
- Broken Squares
- Brainstorm 'How can children and adults get on better?'
- Possibility tree

Week five

Aim: promote creative thinking/co-operation
Activities: warm-up 'affirming circle'
- Human machines
- Who is Mr/Mrs Brown?
- Rain forest

Week six

Aim: creative problem solving
Activities: warm-up 'I love you, honey, but I just can't smile . . .'
 – Phone-in
 – Negotiated agreement – topic 'School Rules'
 – Evaluation so far

Weeks 7/8/9 – Workshops planned by pupils

Aim: to foster and develop affirmation, communication, co-operation and problem solving skills.
Activities: large co-operative picture representing group work. Re-organisation of dinner times to enable all years to feel the system was operating fairly. Warm-ups included 'zoom' and 'paperbacks' and 'I love you, honey . . .'

Each workshop ended with the author and the head of year evaluating the effect of the workshop session on each individual pupil. The next week's workshop was planned and agreed upon, taking these individual needs into account. The head of year discussed with the pupils' tutors the work that had been done during the sessions and this ensured that work done during the workshops was reinforced and followed up in tutorial times.

Evaluation

The children's views

The final session was a de-briefing evaluation enabling each child to make comments about the group and whether they had found it helpful or not. Their responses were transcribed to dictation, hand-written or tape-recorded – depending on pupil preference. All were discussed with the author to check that their comments had been correctly understood. Some of their comments are represented here.

D (a child abuse victim) – 'If you get two sides of the story you can work out what is good . . . Before you start fighting find out the other sides of the story. Enjoyed the co-operative picture, making a mess was good.'

K (a child abuse victim) – 'Have liked it all. It has all been good. Learnt how to listen to other sides of the story, to help someone out if they have a problem, to talk together if people have problems, to listen properly. Liked being in a small group as it is easier to get to know them. Sometimes silly, but then so am I. We enjoyed it.'

I (very withdrawn pupil) – 'The group made me feel better about myself. I feel part of the group. Have had a bit more chance to take part in running. I feel more outgoing and relaxed with people. I enjoyed working together and enjoyed playing games because they are fun.'

J (abuse victim) – 'Gives you a chance to say stuff. Coming to the group makes me more happy. Enjoyed working together on a picture . . . It was fun. Teaches me to share and makes me not bossy. Made me feel better about myself.'

JM (pupil with very poor self-esteem, very disruptive and attention-seeking) – 'Enjoyed . . . paper-backs. See how people thought that you were. They showed their feelings about you, helped you see that people care about you. Enjoyed coming to the group 'cos we need special help. Felt that the group has helped in a way but that it is embarrassing sometimes. Sometimes easier to get on with teachers now. Understand people a bit more.'

P (in trouble for severe disruption, aggression, violent behaviour) – 'Enjoyed talking importantly about the dining hall . . . Made you feel you were responsible and were saying things about what should happen . . . Being taught to be responsible made me feel better about myself. Enjoyed everything. Mrs M and Mr F helping us, showing what a pain in the butt we have been. Enjoyed helping other people and listening to them. Staff thinking I am more helpful instead of fighting other people. Behaviour problem is going.'

M (anxious and withdrawn, concentration problems) – 'Learnt a lot. Communicating together. Not always getting my own way. Not to butt in when someone else is talking. Teachers listen to me a bit more now. Could be to do with the way I am, as I listen more. Most important thing – good communication, being nicer to people.'

R (rated by staff as disruptive) – 'Fed up about missing cookery. Didn't like any of the activities. Quite cross about having to come to the group. Found it boring. Don't feel people listen to my ideas. Mr F does, but no-one else does. Disappointed that our ideas on assemblies and dinners were not followed through. Feel it is a problem to do with people's attitude to me personally.'

K (considered by staff to be acting-out and disruptive) – 'Pleased with how well it turned out. Liked doing the writing. Liked the warm-up activities. When you are not feeling good it makes you laugh. Liked "Who is Mr Brown?" as enjoyed thinking about what sort of person Dad is. Felt I learnt how to be nice.'

Head of year's evaluation

'All the pupils were from year seven. On average the group met fortnightly but because of holidays on occasions the time between the sessions was longer. The group was often reluctant to be withdrawn from lessons. Initially from Games lessons on a Wednesday afternoon and latterly from Design lessons on Tuesday morning. Re-scheduling taking place due to requests from pupils not to miss Games. This reluctance to be withdrawn from normal timetable lessons was a continuing area of conflict. It made the group different and they were somewhat concerned that they had been singled out. The group was comprised of pupils from a number of different tutor groups. Having acknowledged this, for the most part once the group had been assembled and the tasks set the above-mentioned was soon forgotten.

'The group at first were a little uncertain of my rôle in the group. Knowing my position in school as a senior member of staff, they did find initially some difficulty in seeing me as a "learner" and Mrs M as the leader. The barrier of me being a senior member of staff was soon broken down and I believe I have established a good working relationship with all the members of the group – a relationship which would allow me to walk into difficult situations with them and gain their trust and confidence – which is a terrific aid when dealing with children who have extremes of mood . . .

'I think the cohesiveness of the group would have been improved if we had met on a more frequent basis and group rules established would have been retained or recapped more regularly. I am not sure the children overtly perceived the development that they had achieved or have become a great deal more critically aware of their behaviour, certainly not in the case of JM.

'The project has been a useful insight into some of the active work one can employ with children with social and behavioural difficulties. It has enabled me to be confident to cascade thoughts, theories and practical work to other members of the school staff. It has identified me (a senior member of the staff) with the children of this nature within school and given staff the knowledge that there is someone to support.

'The practices and work used within the Tuesday sessions is of great use in the tutorial situation for all children and it should be my task now to disseminate my experience to other members of staff in the school. I am determined that the experience and insight that I have gained through the project should be developed through the school. I am also convinced I must keep a personal contact with the group, looking to value them wherever possible to support the positive attitude we have begun to develop in them. The sessions may have finished but the work needs to be carried on.'

Educational psychologist's evaluation

The individual pupil de-briefing discussions with the head of year that followed every workshop were used to identify the dynamics of the group's interactions and to plan ways in which we would help the pupils develop their interactional skills. For example, at one of the initial sessions JM (a pupil who was causing havoc amongst school staff with severely disruptive and attention-seeking behaviour) began to laugh in a raucous way, which he quickly developed into a hyena-like baying. The group looked to the author, who was leading the session at the time, to see what the response would be.

JM was allowed centre stage for three minutes or so, then the author used the Quiet Sign and the moment he paused for breath, intervened with 'We have listened quietly to you, JM, now it is our turn. We are going to . . .' and turning away from him quickly led the group into the next activity. The de-briefing gave an opportunity to discuss the fact that JM found the intimacy of the group very hard to cope with and covered his embarrassment with outrageous behaviour. When planning subsequent sessions with the group we took this into account and the head of year made sure he was close enough to JM to offer help and encouragement during workshop activities which might otherwise have made JM feel vulnerable or embarrassed.

Not only did pupils receive help during the workshop sessions, but the liaison and extension work that went on via the head of year's meetings with the tutors reinforced the work of the group and made tutors aware of what was going on and the approaches that were being used.

The head of year's responsibility for directing the pastoral work of the tutor groups provided invaluable support and back-up to the project. There was also a high level of parental liaison in the case of at least two pupils, and the on-going project was probably responsible for preventing the exclusion of one pupil who was involved in a serious incident of causing actual bodily harm out of school early on.

On several grounds the project was deemed to be successful. Much of this success should be attributed to the empathy shown by the head of year to pupils who have emotional and behavioural difficulties. He understood the dynamics of the group and the theory that under-pinned the approach. In other words, he was himself a natural problem-solver who had good communication skills.

It became apparent to the author, after only a few sessions, that for some pupils in the group at least, the workshop sessions were having a marked effect. Even on occasions when the author was concerned that on-task behaviour was not maintained for the full session by one or two of the group, the head of year was able to feed back the fact that their involvement, even at this level, was a dramatic improvement on their normal classroom behaviour.

By the end of the project in May both the author and the head of year were pleased with the outcome, feeling that the pupils involved had made positive gains in terms of their communication skills, both speaking and listening; that they had developed a good understanding of what was meant by co-operative working; and that most of them were feeling better about themselves and their situation in school.

Only R felt that he had gained little from the project. Even in this case the pupil's own perceptions contrasted very markedly with the co-worker's views. He had shown himself to have good ideas and to have some leadership skills which could be fostered and developed. His negative anti-social behaviour had previously led him into serious conflicts with many members of staff. We took the view that much of his disruption was due to frustration. An outcome of the sessions was to flag up his potential with other members of staff.

At the end of July the school's special needs teacher gave some additional feed-back. She reported that at the end of the project (the beginning of May) staff in general had not noticed any marked effects of the intervention in school, but that by July all staff were commenting on the changes they had noticed in the pupils concerned. Even pupil R was reluctantly obliged to acknowledge the benefits following his move to a higher academic group.

The success of the first phase of the project has been underlined by the school's commitment to run phase two, with the group to be led by the head of year with another member of staff as co-worker. There is also the expressed intention to use conflict management techniques as part of their personal and social education programme, as well as giving extra support to small groups of pupils who have particular difficulties.

Conclusions

The project fulfilled and exceeded its initial aims and has proved a successful and cost-effective way of offering schools a way of bringing about change in the interactions of pupils with emotional and behavioural difficulties.

Some of the major problems were concerned with time-tabling and having the programme broken by a holiday period. These limitations can be overcome in future work. There is some evidence that the positive experience of one school has encouraged other schools to risk exchanging more traditional ways of working for this type of approach. Conflict management has a broad appeal in that the theory behind the strategies is easily understood by staff and pupils alike. This type of initiative can be run in a variety of different settings. This particular project involved only nine pupils initially in the first cohort of group work. The second cohort also involved nine pupils but this time was run by the year head and supported by a second year head who was also a key stage leader. In this way the strategies could be cascaded through the pastoral tutors of both years. Gradually all pupils within the school will be better equipped to deal with a whole range of problems and stresses in their lives. The staff have continued to be positive about the approach.

Targeting small needy groups initially is only one way to introduce skills based support to children who are experiencing stress and distress in school.

This type of approach, which focuses on training in conciliation and mediation, can be helpful in whole class situations, where there have been incidents of bullying or where a child or group of children are having difficulties integrating with their peers. It could form a basis for initiatives to create a friendly playground. All these strategies can be used across age groups in family settings. Incidentally they can be equally useful to enable adult groups to work more harmoniously together, particularly with groups such as school governors, who need to incorporate new members from time to time.

We all experience conflict in our daily lives and can benefit from developing our communication skills and working more co-operatively. Taking the opportunity to recognise strengths in ourselves and others is likely to create a more friendly working atmosphere.

'Children are invariably trying to solve a problem rather than be one. Their solutions are often misguided because their conception

of the problem is faulty or their skills leave much to be desired.'
(Martin Herbert 1985)

Traditional behaviour modification techniques have the disadvantage of being narrowly focused on a few behaviours and
providing structures which are not necessarily generalisable across
situations. Conflict management, on the other hand, uses
strategies which will give children skills to stand them in good
stead, not only at a social interaction level but also in areas of
speaking and listening and group initiatives which are central to
the National Curriculum.

References

Assessment of Performance Unit: Speaking and Listening (1986)
Assessment age 11

Bowers S. Wells L 1987 Ways and means – An approach to problem
solving. The Handbook of Kingston Friends Workshop Group

Evans G 1992 *Child protection a whole curriculum approach*. Avec Designs
Ltd

Dunne E. Bennett N 1990 *Talking and learning in groups*. Leverhulme
Primary Project

Faupel A W A 1990 Model response to emotional and behavioural
development in schools. *Educational Psychology in Practice* 5(4)

Herbert. M 1985 *Caring for your children*. Blackwells

HMI 1989b *Aspects of primary education – teaching and learning of science*.
HMSO London

McConnon S 1989 *The skills of friendship*. Macmillan Education

Maines B. Robinson G 1992 *Michael's story. The no blame approach*. Lame
Duck Publishing

Moon A 1990 *Skills for the primary school child*. TACADE

National Oracy Project 1989 Talk: the Journal of the National Oracy
Project No 1 London: NCC (1989)

National Curriculum Council)/HMSO 1989 *English in the National
Curriculum Key Stage 1.*

Ross C. Ryan A 1991 *Can I stay in today, Miss? Improving the school
playground*. Trentham Books

Saunders L 1989 Report of a study on conflict management in the
classroom. ISTD and KFWG

Scott D H. Marston W C 1971 *Bristol social adjustment guides*. Hodder &
Stoughton Ltd

Appendix

WORKSHOP RECORD

Run by: ....TM.............................. Date:.....22-1-91......

with: ....SF................................

Time: ....

Aim of Session: ..No. 4 Improving Communication/Co-operation..

Materials needed:

1 ...Broken Squares............... 4 ....

2 ...Flipchart..................... 5 ....
   Plastic envelopes (7)
3 ...for clipboards............... 6 ....

ACTIVITIES	BRIEF EVALUATION
1 Zoom 'warm-up Page 126	Activity enjoyed by the whole group. P wanted answers to questions before explanation has finished. All enjoyed having the power to control the game.
2 Broken Squares Page 63	An exercise the first group found difficult. Involvement was sporadic – attention was seized for 5 minutes or so. Sharing was difficult. JM found this very difficult, and did not know how to handle this and the
3	result was he made noises and comments to avoid embarrassment. Some observers esp. R could not avoid joining in – talking was inevitable as communication was difficult.
4 Brainstorm "How can adults and children get on better?"	Brainstorm was received well and all contributed to the group effort. Comments after referred to what parents could give to children and not vice versa. Suggestions did widen to shared things but had to be led
5 Recording	towards thinking what they could give to parents. Recording of the brainstorm was the worst received activity and this may be due to the group's poor recording skills.

Evaluation of Session:

OBSERVERS' NOTES FOR BROKEN SQUARES

Each person has an envelope containing pieces for forming squares. At the signal, the task of the group is to form five equally sized, perfect squares, one in front of each person. There is no speaking, and no taking of pieces from each other, but pieces can be offered and accepted.

Points for observation during the game
(a)   Is everybody involved?
Sporadically – Involvement for short length of time – concentration lapse.

(b)   What happened to the person who began the game with only one piece?
Just sat at first. Then offered it to nearest person. This started some swapping – left K without for a while.

(c)   Did you notice people starting to help each other?
Yes. Soon started to help each other.

(d)   Of those who completed a square early in the game:
  –   did anyone sit back and not bother any more?
  Most were interested in the activity

  –   did anyone offer to break it up to complete someone else's?
  Yes eventually – one person gave up a square.

(e)   Of those who completed a square late in the game:
  –   did anyone seem worried?
  No-one seemed unduly worried.

  –   did anyone opt out?
  Not for any length of time.

(f)   Anything else of interest?
Talking started – observers wanting to get involved completed square. Owners looked for diversions. Noises and comments to hide embarrassment at not being able to complete task. Group began to split into smaller groups.

WORKSHOP RECORD

Run by   TM
                                        Date ...12.11.90......
  with   SF

Time   2.00–3.15 pm

Aim of session ....“Getting to know you” session. Setting the
.....................scene and explaining ground rules.

Materials needed:

1. *Self adhesive labels/Marker pens
2. Dictionaries/thesauri
3. *Bulldog clips/*Flip chart
4. Drawing paper

5. Scissors, selotape, glue
6. Worksheets/evaluation sheets
7. *Box for materials
8. 1 or 2 large cardboard boxes; enough pieces of stiff card for each pupil to make a clipboard

Activities	Brief evaluation
Naming – each group member shares something about their name.	This activity went well and was a good ice-breaker.
Names – using dictionaries/thesauri and the letters in your name find words which describe you: J – jolly, just; A – angelic, aggressive?; N – noisy, nuisance, nice; E – etc.	An activity which did not depend on literacy skills would have been better. The group found dictionary work hard
Write name on label and draw picture which shows something about yourself.	Group enjoyed this activity and were very creative when representing their own identity and interests.
Use information about ‘self’ for clip board decoration. Use name and descriptions of self and drawings to decorate board which will be used to keep worksheets and evaluations together over the weeks.	Good start made on clip boards using information stated on name labels. Will continue next week.
Share information with group and complete ‘feelings maps’.	No time for this activity so postponed to week 2.

Evaluation of session:

*Can be supplied by TM. Helpful if other items can be available in school. Any problems please contact TM prior to session (preferably Friday 9 November).

WORKSHOP RECORD

Date ...28.11.90.......

Run by   TM..................................

with   SF..................................

Time   2.00–3.15 pm.........................

Aim of session ......No. 2 – Co-operative activities/Feelings........

Materials needed:

1. Bulldog clips............................   5. Prompt sheet ....

2. Glue/scissors............................   6. ....

3. Large paper for picture................   7. ....

4. Art materials/bits......................   8. ....

Activities	Brief evaluation
Warm-up "Paper backs"	Group enjoyed the positive feedback and thanked other group members for their comments.
Finish Clip boards (rehearse ground rules)	Clipboards that are finished have turned out well. Rest to be completed in tutor time.
Co-operative picture theme – Christmas Prompts: time/size/materials/subject	Theme delayed as 4 opted out of group due to house matches. Agreed that group who came would continue activities with rest during tutor time – all to experience 'paper-backs', 'feelings' maps.
Feelings maps	Group enjoyed this activity and suggested that they number their maps so that they know which session they applied to.

Evaluation of session:

WORKSHOP RECORD

Revised date ....28.11.90..........

Run by   TM...................................

with   SF....................................

Time   2.00–3.15 pm...................

Aim of session ....No. 3 – Listening skills........................

....

Materials needed:

1. Flipchart (TMcC)............................. 5. ....

2. Clipboards....................................... 6. ....

3. Paper/writing materials................... 7. ....

4. .... 8. ....

Activities	Brief evaluation
1. Quicklist "What makes a good listener?"	"Listening" warm-up disrupted by P. Did contribute to quicklist. JM very attention-seeking throughout. Concensus that listening to others' contributions important.
2. Listening for feelings "Support or Sabotage?" – cruel and out of date or a Great British tradition?	"Listening" to two viewpoints reasonable. Asking group to take 'other' viewpoint *very* difficult for some especially P, who found it impossible. Others such as M made a good effort at taking opposing view to his own. Observers also had some problems, especially K.
3. Discussion	P agreed taking someone else's point of view difficult. JM was embarrassed working with group and was quite disruptive (noisy laughing). Waiting whilst he calmed down and telling him we had listened to his display, now it was time to give others a chance surprised him. R opted out.
4. "The Maligned Wolf Story" Page 79	K wanted to read the story. She became progressively more attention-seeking from this point on but read the story well and made positive contributions. They all agreed that it was important to listen to the 'other side'. Volunteering other stories which only present one view.
5. "I messages..." Page 109	Discussion on this went well. Apart from K flirting with JM and J being attention-seeking session went well. I may need more help to feel part of group. J, despite reluctance to join initially, had finished his flip-chart by the end.

Evaluation of session:
The co-hesion of the group had been somewhat lost over the holiday and we may need to do more work on this next time. P, although finding the listening tasks hard, did make a contribution to the group. J was very attention-seeking throughout. D showed enormous improvement and was actively contributing to activities. A notable change. Others need help to feel the group is 'theirs' also.

WORKSHOP RECORD

Date ....22.1.91.........

Run by   TM..................................

with   SF..................................

Time   ....

Aim of session ...No. 4 – Improving Communication/Co-operation.

....

Materials needed:

1. Broken squares (TMcC)............   5.................................

2. Flipchart (for possibility tree)......   6.................................

3. ....Plastic envelopes (7) for........   7.................................

4. ....clipboards (SF)..................   8.................................

Activities	Brief evaluation
1. Zoom (warm-up) Page 126	Slow to get going on this – rather 'unusual' task for them so rather inhibited. Will repeat and they may then enjoy it more. Two said they thought this task OK; 6 said it was good. 6 pupils listed it as something they enjoyed.
2. Broken squares Page 62	All the group reported enjoying this task. Some said it taught them sharing, some reported that they had found it hard. We ran through it twice with observers and participants alternating. The 2nd run through was done much more co-operatively and each ended up with a finished square.
3. Brainstorm "How can adults and children get on better?"	The brainstorm was recorded by K and K who coped well with minimal prompting. They were a bit short on balance tending to opt for things *they* wanted, focused more appropriately on caring and sharing when they came to record what they thought was important.
4. Possibility Tree Page 123	This was not done – we used the brainstorm information and they had free choice as to how it was recorded. Some very creative responses. All except JM had chosen very individual ways of recording.
5.	

Evaluation of session:

All beginning to get something meaningful out of the group. Even off-task behaviour not disruptive. JM's low s/e is preventing him from enjoying himself as much as the others. He will need more help next time.

WORKSHOP RECORD

Date ...5.3.91.........

Run by ....TM with SF........................

Time ....

Aim of session ..No. 6 – Problem Solving.....................

Materials needed:

1. .Tape recorders..........................   4. ....

2. .Tapes...................................   5. ....

3. .Flipchart for brainstorm..............   6. ....

Activities	Brief evaluation
1. (Warm-up) "I love you, honey, but I just can't smile..." Round groups – see how many can say it without!	Group enjoyed this activity, and no-one managed a straight face, including SF and myself!
2. "Phone-in" Tape record problems then swap for recorded reply.	This activity went well on the whole & provoked discussion. However, the pupils needed help with the recorders & were embarrassed at sharing problems & so this delayed them getting into it. A second try at this type of activity would go better. The whole group discussion generated some thoughtful & supportive ideas.
3. "Negotiated agreement" Topic – "School Rules"	This provoked a lively discussion of the dinner arrangements & a brainstorm of improvement suggestions. The group were enthusiastic about taking the ideas to the Head & School Council, but were still unsure as to whether their suggestions would be valued.
4. Evaluation (a) Feelings maps (6 wks) (b) What I liked best (up to 5 activities) (c) What I have achieved (not shared with group)	A school newspaper/news-sheet/noticeboard was also discussed and this and topic 3 are to be negotiated and planned over the next sessions. The group will finish their evaluations as part of this work.
5. With SF plan 19.3.91 26.3.91 23.4.91	The Tuesday group to discuss and plan the next three sessions. I will organise the starting warm-up and a finishing activity on each session.

Evaluation of session: The session was lively and went well. Towards the end, the group had used up their concentration. In future we will have an ending activity to help draw the group together. "Unusual" activities need practice with this type of group and they often benefit from a repeat try at some activities.

Mr Stinking chair
Just sitting there
In a room

Mr Stinking tape
Playing on my mind
Silly scratched record
Your itch is hard to find

Chains of fear
Keep him near
Pale faced man
Takes away what's dear

Amen

John Green
November 1992

Index

The man on a bike his name is Mike
But to you this man's just a man on a bike.
He has his own little life separate from yours.
He's typing words while you're doing your chores.

The man could be lonely could be sitting alone
He talks to himself while you're on the phone.
He bottles up his worries
When you moan and groan.

The man on a bike so cheery but old
Alone by the fire protected from cold.
He's sad and recalls the days of old
The wireless, the long johns, evacuation and all,
And he remembers the soldiers, especially Paul.

He has a past and you have a future
You have warm teachers instead of cold tutors.

John Green
1992